A SAVAGE LIFE

A SAVAGE LIFE

MICHAEL SAVAGE

WILLIAM MORROW
An Imprint of HarperCollinsPublishers

For Janet Roll Weiner, who has watched over me as
a guardian angel

All memories are traces of tears.

CHINESE PROVERB

CONTENTS

INTRODUCTION

I REALLY WAS POOR!

AT MY RECENT BIRTHDAY PARTY, MY SON GOT UP TO GIVE A little speech about his dad, and he mentioned something intriguing. Here's what he said: "When my dad told me that he was so poor when he was young that he actually wore a dead man's pants, I thought he was just exaggerating as I often think he does. But tonight before the party, he showed me childhood pictures that were just sent to him from relatives for this book. I was astounded to see he actually was wearing pants, hand-me-downs, five times too large, cut off at the knee. I couldn't believe his family was actually that poor."

Well, that's the end of that quote. In reviewing the photographs in this book, you will see that exact picture: me standing beneath my aunt, straddled by my sister and my cousin, wearing dead man's pants. Every word that you read in this book is as true as that photograph.

IN GOING THROUGH PHOTOGRAPHS FOR THIS BOOK, I FOUND pictures of many of the men that I write about: the gambler, the leather man, the uncle who was a Democratic Party operative. What strikes me is that they were all very ordinary-looking men. You would never pick them out of a crowd and think they were anything special. And that's just the point of this book, which is that in the ordinary there is the extraordinary. Now, whether it is that men were more dynamic in those days, or that I saw the dynamism in their lives, is for anyone to guess. I don't know. Are men still like that? There is a movie called *The Naked City* where it is said, "There are eight million stories in the naked city. This has been one of them." I was fascinated by that as a young boy, because it showed me that every individual person walking the streets had a story, if only you could find that story. And all of my life I've found this to be true, that of course every human in their destiny, in their journey through life, is actually weaving a story. It's just that most of us don't even realize we are unique or weaving a story. Or is it that the times have made so many of us homogenous? Have we become just one massive group of individuals in a sort of socialist hive? Well, whatever the case may be, *A Savage Life* contains the stories of ordinary men and women, each of whom was extraordinary.

ONE

TRAIN TRACKS

I ATTENDED GRADE SCHOOL IN BRONX, NEW YORK, IN THE late 1940s, early 1950s. What I remember most was my mom coming to school on a Wednesday before the Thanksgiving weekend and picking us up early in the day, before the other kids were let out, and taking me and my sister down to Manhattan to Penn Station to board a train to visit my cousins, my aunt, and my uncle in Easton, Pennsylvania. My father, of course, couldn't come with us; he had to stay and work. He worked seven days a week in his store. Thanksgiving vacations with my relatives in Pennsylvania were perhaps the most American part of my early childhood.

How exciting it was to be getting out of school early

on a Wednesday and seeing all the other jealous faces of the kids left behind! Mom would take us downtown by bus and by subway, and it was thrilling to get into Penn Station: the big hissing trains—the size of the train, the engine in particular—overwhelming me as a little boy. It looked like a hippopotamus, a living, breathing monster. And then boarding the train: the black men with white gloves in white clothing who worked as porters. Astounding, isn't it? And then the train would begin, a long ride to me; it was only two hours or so, but to me it was a very, very long ride. An hour or so seemed like it took all day. The train chugged underneath the Hudson River into New Jersey and, believe it or not, the train stopped on the other side of the river. It stopped to switch engines. You see, only electric engines were permitted in New York, but in those days New Jersey still permitted coal-fired steam engines, if you can believe it. And so the railroad companies switched to coal-fired, steam-driven locomotives over in New Jersey, and then the entire ride from that point on was bathed in a dense black smoke that ran behind the train, between the cars, outside the windows, all the way to Pennsylvania.

Ah, but sitting in that Pullman car, being served those delicious ham sandwiches with mayonnaise on white bread by white-gloved attendants . . . Can you believe it? Even a poor kid could experience a sense of dignity in those days. And then when we arrived in Pennsylvania at the station, when the big monstrous train hissed to a stop and roared, emitting steam and smoke, the entire platform was engulfed in black smoke and white steam, and I didn't know if my relatives were there because you couldn't see anybody in that fog. It was such a dense fog. I was afraid that the train had gone to the wrong place, to an unknown place, and that none of our relatives would be there. And my mother would hold me by the hand and pull me through the fog. And then of course! As the fog lifted, out of the fog came the big uncle and the smiling aunt and my smiling cousins. Oh my god, was that happiness.

We would jump in their car and the first thing we would do was go to a certain restaurant on top of a hill, overlooking the town of Pittston, where it was alleged their hamburger was actually horse meat. We didn't learn this until years later, but I must tell you, as a poor kid I didn't know the difference between horse meat and cow meat. It tasted a little stringy, to be honest, but maybe that's what makes me the man I am today. In any case, one memory after another comes back from those Thanksgiving holidays in Pennsylvania with my cousins. Memories like and unlike those that you, the reader, no doubt have of your own. Shall I share a few of them with you?

How about learning how to drive a stick shift in the little Nash Metropolitan that my cousin owned (a tiny little car that looked like a clown car) and the mysteriousness of shifting? I didn't understand where the gears were or what they did. And I was amazed and thought that my cousin was an astronaut as he shifted from first to second to third, pushing his foot down against the floor. I had no idea what the shift levers were doing. But we'd drive all around the town. You see, he was about sixteen and allowed to drive at that time.

Or how about he and I putting on all of the football gear, the shoulder pads, the knee pads, the helmet, and playing football in the muddy field across from his house? This was a big football town in those days; in fact, a game between Easton, Pennsylvania, and I think it was Pittstown, New Jersey, was the big high school game. And we'd all go and cheer; it must've been on a Sunday. But before that game, oh, my cousin and I were the stars. We were the stars among ourselves. I remember running all day, running as though there was no time, slipping and falling in the mud until we looked like the mud itself. Coming back to the house, being shooed in through the back door because we were so dirty, being told to leave our clothing on the back porch—and it was so cold.

Speaking of the cold, I remember their dog. They had a beautiful, collie-like dog whose fur always smelled of the cold air. You know how dogs smell on a cold day, how they retain the cold as they come in? I loved to touch that dog. We weren't allowed to have a dog in those days because of the apartment that we had. So to me, it was miraculous to see a family living in an actual house of two stories with an attic and a basement and a dog.

It was in that little house on Spring Garden Street that I smelled my first pizza. You say, What the heck is the big deal about that? *Well,* let me tell you something. I was upstairs in the attic getting ready for bed and I heard all the people buzzing downstairs in the kitchen about something. We came down and peeked around the corner and they were all looking at something in a box, a flat box. It was called a pizza. I didn't know what it was, but you know what it smelled like? Vomit. That's what mozzarella cheese first smelled like to me. Who knows if this perception was accurate or if, in fact, mozzarella cheese was just terrible in those days. In either case, it was something I could not eat. They sure liked it, though, that "first pizza."

I remember my uncle Abe, a sweet, tall man, my mother's brother. They had left New York City so he could take a job during the Depression, working as a hand in a brassiere factory in Pennsylvania. You may laugh at this, but that's what people had to do in those days to survive. He was a sweet-hearted, lovable, big fellow like a Max Baer–type, always friendly, always a smile for everyone. And as it turned out, Abe was quite the local political figure. I had no idea at the time, but as the years progressed, he got himself deeply involved in local Democratic Party politics.

Abe was an amazing man in many ways, a powerful personality who functioned in a variety of ways and on multiple levels, as all of us do. He was an infuriated ward leader, is what he turned out to be. He certainly symbolized the old-fashioned ward boss, but beneath that gruff exterior was my sweet uncle. He was amazingly devoted to his family and friends. It was said that he never said no to anyone asking him for a favor. You see, he had been steeled in adversity, not in diversity. He was born in Montreal, Canada, in 1911 and raised in New York City in great hardship. As I said, he settled in Easton, Pennsylvania, where he started as a factory hand and moved up to being factory foreman, and nevertheless still struggled. As time went on he went into the political sphere and his life greatly improved. This is a part of the obituary that was written in the local newspaper:

> *Abe Cohen, dead at 71: Abe Cohen, a familiar figure in his houndstooth hat, who politicians say delivered votes as regularly as the post office does mail, died Saturday. Mr. Cohen, age 71, was pronounced dead on arrival at Easton Hospital. He died of natural causes. He celebrated his 50th wedding anniversary*

with his wife on June 23rd. He made a name for himself in the local political scene. For more than 30 years he was a Democratic Committeeman in Easton's 8th Ward, Western District, where he lived. He also headed campaigns for various state senators several times, and also for the mayor. He was a member of the local Zoning Board and was involved in several zoning controversies in the past few years. Quote: "He was so outspoken. He told you the truth," said one of the managers of the city parking garage who waged successful campaigns for mayor in '71 and '75. "Abie always told you where you stood." The ex-mayor said Mr. Cohen liked to call himself "the old-time politician." His associates said he was a good one. On Election Day he was not interested in money. He was interested in bringing out the votes, said people who had worked with him.

Anyway, it's interesting to see that he was an old-time politician and, by what I can read in this obituary, deeply involved in tussles—for example, he seemed at one time to have backed the only Republican in a Democratic factory town, and for that he was thrown off a local zoning board for over two years. In fact, he was removed from his zoning board seat in 1977 and reappointed to the board only two years later. And then he got even with the man

who got him thrown off the zoning board. I had no idea
he was this political, but I can see there must be some political blood running through the family somewhere. He
was the only one I knew who actually did any politics. It
says elsewhere in this obituary, "If a constituent wanted
something in Abe's ward, he went to Abe. Abe would go
to no end to help these people. Time has changed, bringing a new breed of politician that wasn't so quick to hand
out patronage jobs. It became just as easy to harvest votes
through the media. The Abe Cohens lost clout but there
was a time when many politicians wouldn't whisper such
a thing . . . He retired at the end of his career as a special
investigator for the Pennsylvania Department of Revenue
Bureau of Cigarette and Beverage Taxes. He was named
to the post by the administration of the Democrat Governor after he led the Governor's successful campaign in that
town. From 1931 to 1952 he was a mere cutter in an under-
wear factory. From '52 to '71 he was in another factory job,
a pocketbook factory."

I had no idea that I had such a political uncle. But I
can say to you, this whole book, *Train Tracks*, is about the
train tracks that run from my childhood right through my
quasi-political career of today. Although I am not involved
in politics in any direct manner—I never have and never
will run for office—I am certainly anything but apolitical.

Nevertheless, other memories include his wife, my

aunt, and her famous meringue pie, something I have never seen in New York City. I didn't eat it because I don't like sugary things, but it was certainly beautiful to look at it and truly a part of an American dream that I had never seen in a small tenement apartment in New York. The idea of baking a pie or baking a cake was not something that we got in my beautiful home, where my mother cooked but didn't bake. Other memories to follow in *Train Tracks*.

Living in a crowded apartment as we did, it was a real treat to run around the two-story house in Pennsylvania. I loved the attic, I loved sleeping in the attic—there was something mysterious and secretive about it. I especially loved their basement. It was not one of those "finished" basements. It was an open basement that was always cold and damp, as basements are. But they had built shelves in the basement. And on these shelves were canned goods. It looked to me like a grocery store itself: the long rows of Campbell's soups, the long rows of spaghetti, long rows of canned sauces and other packaged foods. To us it was a cornucopia. Most interesting to me as a kid was a well-oiled Japanese rifle that my cousin's uncle from the other side of his family had brought home as a souvenir from World War II. Apparently he had served in Japan and brought home a Japanese rifle, which I played with, opening and closing the bolt and pulling the trigger as often as I could. I loved the sound of the bolt. I loved the sound as I pulled the trigger. I loved the smell of the grease that was in the gun to preserve it. I loved the feel of the wood stock. I loved the blue of the barrel. I guess I've always loved guns.

Ever since those times, I've been infatuated by trains. Although I don't ride the rails any longer, I remember up until the late 1970s and early '80s out here in California I would as often as possible, which was probably only three or four times a year, escape from all of my responsibilities and worries and board an Amtrak train over in the East Bay and ride it up to Lake Tahoe, getting off at Truckee, California. It was just as magical in those days as it was back in my childhood days—in this case, in some ways more dramatic because I understood the beauty of the rails. I remember especially the motion of the train, standing between the cars, which you were allowed to do at that time, inhaling the air, watching the countryside zip by. Perhaps most beautiful was when we entered the mountains of the High Sierra, the deep granite mountains, where the railroad tunnels were blasted out a century before. Those were simply amazing, coming out of the tunnel into the snowcapped mountains of the High Sierra Nevada, ending up at Truckee, California, an old mountain railroad town that, to this day, retains its rustic charm.

TWO

BOY IN THE RIVER

NOTICE THE PHOTO OF MY FATHER STANDING IN THE Neversink River in the Catskill Mountains.* He was a young man then and I was about three or four years old. An incident occurred then that has shaped my life. There was a large waterfall not far from there that we kids were warned to avoid. South Fallsburg, New York, was the location. My dad and I were upriver, me in a large inner tube splashing around, protected by my father, or so I thought. He began to maneuver the tube so I was upriver from him and the waterfall, with the strong current running to-

---

* See interior photo insert.

wards him and down, down, down to the churning white falls. As he pushed me away from him, and away from the direction of the waterfall, he said, "I'm pushing you over the falls." And with a smile he pushed me. I began to cry. In fact I lost my little head, fearing he was sending me to my death! As the current took me towards him he grabbed on to my tube and said, "Don't worry, I was just kidding."

Since then I have never completely trusted anyone. Maybe he did me a favor, knowing people and the world. Maybe he did this because he wanted to toughen me up. Who really knows? But this was my Abraham-and-Isaac moment. And I don't think it was God who told him to fake pushing me over the waterfall only to tell him not to at the last moment.

THREE

THE PORCH

THE TITLE OF THIS BOOK IS *TRAIN TRACKS*, BUT IT REALLY could have been *Wheels*. Today, I'm riding on my bicycle and pass a house with a small lawn mower manufactured by Honda. And my mind goes back along the train tracks in my mind, to my boyhood in a little attached house in Queens, New York, where we had a Briggs & Stratton lawn mower. Hey, "the times they are a-changing," huh? That's right, an American mower, Briggs & Stratton. How I loved that little lawn mower when I used to pull the cord on it. I had to pull it a few times to get it started, and then when it would choke and spit and cough, then fire up, how great it was to go around our little tiny backyard.

But I'm reminded of the little porch that my father built, attached to our little brick house. How proud he was of that porch! I have no idea where he learned the skills to do it. Now, it wasn't exactly a major house that he built, but he did have a concrete foundation poured, he was careful to insert the foundation screws into the cement, and he explained to me how these would be used to attach to the main support beams of the little porch. Everything worked out fine. I remember it was red cement and how it was grooved with intricate designs, and how slowly he built up the sides to about four feet in height, and then above the four-foot sides there were screens all around and, of course, a little sloped roof. I spent many of my adolescent nights, hot summer nights, sleeping on a couch out on that porch, wondering about many things, including where the train tracks of my mind would take me in the future.

While it's not unusual for men in the Midwest to know how to build things, it's quite unusual, in my mind at least, to imagine how an immigrant who was a small shop-keeper knew how to do any of these basic building things. I don't know where he learned it from. I don't know how he learned how to use tools. Perhaps men of that generation were more versatile in their abilities. Nevertheless, when he died, the basement was found to be filled with a great old workbench that he had bought from some carpenter, various and sundry brass tools and iron tools, some of which I've kept to this day, including pipe wrenches made of brass, right-angle irons made of copper or brass—just beautiful, almost antique instruments by today's plastic comparison.

FOUR

CARS

"So round. So firm. So fully packed." Well, if you can believe it, that was the signature ad for a major cigarette brand in the 1950s when I was growing up. Obviously they were describing more than a cigarette. But nevertheless, that slogan seems to have typified cars as well as cigarettes. In fact, the shape of cars in my formative years took on the shape of many of the buxom women on the screens in theaters throughout America. We all know about the Dagmar bumpers of the Cadillacs.

My first car, which remains my favorite car, was a dark green, 1955 Oldsmobile, two-door "salesman's coupe." Naturally, I loved the car, but I wished that it was a two-door hardtop rather than a salesman's coupe. But beggars can't be choosers. I remember when my dad drove it home for me, parked it outside our little attached house on Utopia Parkway in Queens, New York. It was a rainy night. I went and sat inside the car without even starting the engine. I must have sat there for hours. I remember that night very vividly. Raindrops beading on the windshield.

If you look at the pictures in this book, you'll see my dad standing next to a dark green, '54 or '55 Cadillac Sedan Deville, his car at that time. Naturally, both his car and mine were used cars, in that we couldn't afford a new one; and he refused to buy anything "on time." That's right, he thought that buying something on credit was cheating and faking it for your neighbors and friends. He said if you couldn't afford to pay cash for a car, it meant that you were living way beyond your means.

I don't know if cars still have the same power or meaning for people today. I certainly am still somewhat of a car nut. I have several different ones, including a 1965 red Cadillac convertible, which still has very low mileage, about 55,000 miles. In fact, I bought it soon after starting in radio in 1994 and have hardly driven it since then. It sits in the garage, taking up nineteen feet and six inches of space for no good reason.

FIVE

Food

I don't think I ate a grain of rice in my childhood. It was all pasta and potatoes. Oh, how much rice I've eaten since then! Rice, rice, rice. Chinese, Chinese, Japanese, Japanese, Thai, Thai, Chinese, Japanese. Oh, how times have changed.

Food is certainly a big part of anyone's life. In my case, it's a bigger part of my life than I'd like to admit. I knew a man once, a very fine man, an art dealer and historian from London, who helped fund my research to the Fiji Islands when the government wouldn't do so because I was thirty years ahead of my time. I was doing ethnobotanical research. The government said, "*Nyet*, no, we don't fund such craziness."

Of course, today it's all *en vogue*.

So I funded it myself, and when I needed extra help I would go to this gentleman. I remember as I got to know him over the years, he said to me, "You know, when I was a young man all I thought about was women. As I got older," he said, "I would drive across London or Paris for a new restaurant I heard about."

Well, that about summarizes it.

My mother, God bless her, spent her last years in an assisted living facility in Boca Raton, Florida. Well, all I heard about was food, food, food—how bad the food was. I'll never forget, when I arranged to have food delivered for her from local Chinese or Italian restaurants, I had to hire a taxicab. After her complaining to me for over a year about how bad the food was at the facility, I remember looking up a taxi company, arranging with the taxi driver, and he drove her Chinese food and then he drove her Italian food, and all she would say was, it was not too good. It wasn't good this way or that way, compared to New York.

About six months later I found out that both that Chinese restaurant and the Italian restaurant that I bothered to find a cabdriver to deliver for, delivered directly for no charge whatsoever! I guess that's mothers and sons for you, and that's why I say, food has always played a bigger role in my life than I'd like to admit.

SIX

"Nite Club"

The bar was dark, like a scene out of *The Godfather*. We sat next to the long, dark mahogany bar at a small table. The steak was served. I had never eaten steak that was this soft. In fact, I didn't know that steak was supposed to be soft. The only steaks I had ever eaten before were hard, rubbery, difficult to cut. This one cut like butter. The tough man served us without a smile. We were the only ones in there on a Saturday afternoon. It was on the Upper East Side of Manhattan in what was known as Yorktown, a German neighborhood. It was owned by my friend's father, Jackie Hart, who was the toughest guy in the neighborhood. He was a professional gambler and a club owner, long before anyone knew what that meant.

All the other men were either small businessmen with tiny little stores, or they worked in the trades or in the garment center. Jackie was a guy out of *The Godfather*. He was quiet. He hardly ever spoke. Everyone respected him and everyone feared him. We had gotten downtown not by train tracks, but one of the hard men from the bar had come to get us by car, to eat in Jackie's bar. There are many stories about Jackie; this was one of them, the one about the soft steak served by the hard man.

Another story about Jackie that comes to mind occurred around the same period when I was seven, eight, nine years old, in the Catskill Mountains, where most of the families from our apartment building retreated to what were known as bungalow colonies, in essence small villages that were rented for the summer. Each family rented a small cottage. This was paradise lost. One summer, my family, Jackie's family, probably ten others, all rented individual cottages or bungalows at the same place. It was on a long, sloping, grassy hill with a swimming pool. This summer a huge fight had broken out between the owners of the bungalow colony and this group from the Bronx. It was very unusual for these men to engage in a fight, but fight they did. It started over an insult thrown at one of our neighboring women by the owner in the little grocery store that belonged to and was run by the bungalow colony owner. Who knows what it was over, but it was a huge fight that went on for most of the day and it ended up with Fat Pat the Bookie dragging one of the brothers around the property by his collar, pulling him until he gave up, but he wouldn't give up. Fat Pat kept pulling him around, telling him, "It's time you gave up," but the guy wouldn't give up. Jackie Hart, on the other hand, got into a fistfight with one of them and bashed the guy's head in. The guy bit him in the forearm and as you may know, human bites are far more deadly than dog bites. It took him months for that wound to heal.

Jackie was a street fighter long before he was a bar owner, growing up in the Yorktown area of New York. He told a story years later to us young kids about the period during World War II when there was an actual Nazi party in New York City and other places, sympathetic to Hitler. Jackie was on a subway car when one of the American Nazis jumped up and started to scream, "Kill the Jews! Kill the Jews! Kill the Jews!" Jackie was not a man given to words. He didn't react with words. He said he waited until the subway car stopped at a train station. He grabbed the man and smashed his head between the car and the platform until he was a bloody pulp, and then he left without a word. That was Jackie Hart.

There was a fight he talked about from his childhood

that landed him in the hospital for over six months. He'd gotten into a fight with a guy he called the toughest man he ever met in his life. Who knows what it was over. Who knows what people fight over to begin with? I don't remember the man's name, but I met him years later and he was absolutely intimidating and frightening, another man of few words. In fact, this other man spoke no words whatsoever. But when you shook this man's hand, even as a little kid, it was like holding a catcher's mitt. It was all calluses. He wouldn't even close his hand for fear he would crush your hand. All he did was smile. He was very devoted to his wife who was very homely. Nevertheless, this man who had beaten Jackie when he was a boy—and they had gotten into a fight over something, and it landed Jackie in the hospital for several months—this guy came to the hospital every day during his recovery and sat with him even though they hadn't known each other, and then they became lifetime friends.

Years later, as it would turn out, Jackie had a son, my best friend, Davy, who was actually my protector because he was a tough kid, really tough; he wouldn't let anyone do anything to any of his friends. He also had a daughter named Darlene. His daughter went into the arts and she wound up dead from an overdose in a Manhattan hotel. Jackie's wife went to pieces. Not only could she not take care of herself, she couldn't talk, couldn't eat, couldn't cook. There were no psychiatrists in those days, not for poor people. There was no closure in those days, not for poor people. There was just grief and friends, and that's where my saintly mother came in. For weeks and months my mother would go to her apartment, cook for her, bathe her, take care of her, as she slowly got over the death of her daughter.

SEVEN

PROPELLERS

AT SOME POINT IN MY LIFE THE TRAIN TRACKS BECAME propellers—ships' propellers, you see. The fact of the matter is that when I was a young man, driving my old little Volkswagen, a little green Bug, on the West Side Highway, the great ships of the time were lined up on their piers on the Hudson River. Oh, how excited I used to get! I remember thinking, one day I'm going to be on those ships and I'm going to go to Europe and I'm going to join the greats of the world. I'm going to join all of the heroes, all of my literary heroes, with grand adventures and great love affairs, nights at sea under the stars. Oh, those ships used to excite me as I saw them on the piers with their high prows, facing the West Side Highway.

Well, as the years went on, I did sail on many ships. The first one was the MV *Waterman*, the Motor Vessel *Waterman*. I was still in college and I did my big trip to Europe with a friend of mine. It was a converted troop carrier from World War II, and it was quite a tub. It took ten days to go from New York City to Southampton. It was all college kids and, my god, what a time we had. We slept all day and partied all night. One thing I remember most vividly from that voyage was the old Dutchman who shared a cabin with three of us young guys, deep below in the belly of the beast. He was blind, in his eighties. One night I was sick and tired of the partying and I went down into the cabin to talk to the old Dutchman. I remember asking him, "Old man, what's the meaning of life?"

You see, I was one of those kinds of kids. *The Sorrows of Young Werther* comes to mind.

"Oh, old man, what's the meaning of life?"

He stared up at me with his unseeing blue eyes and he repeated my question, "What's the meaning of life? What's the meaning of life?" And as he stared at me with his unblinking eyes, he said, "Well, I guess the meaning of life is you're born holding it and you die holding it."

I've never forgotten that because that's about as close as anyone's ever come to explaining the meaning of life, meaning nobody knows. Nobody knows.

I saw the angel of death . . .

That's right. Not all of my trips at sea were delightful. On one of my trips from Majorca, Spain, to Barcelona, I took a small passenger vessel that held about a hundred and fifty people. Apparently we got caught in a mistral, a small hurricane. The ship was bucking violently and I became violently ill. In fact, I had to go to the deck and lean over the side, I was so sick. I'll never forget, one of the deckhands, a burly guy with a mean face, held me as I leaned over the side, relieving myself of that day's breakfast. As I looked up at the sea, on the bucking rail I saw looming above me a large, winged angel of death. To this day I insist I saw the angel of death. Or was it just plain seasickness, who knows? I just never want to repeat the experience.

Well, since that time I've been on many ships. Some of the names come back to me: the *Royal Viking Sea*, the *Maasdam*, the *Statendam*.

Years later as I traveled from Hawaii, where I was living and studying, to the islands of the South Pacific to do my ethnobotanical research in Fiji, Tonga, Samoa, the Marquesas, I would often travel on the P&O liners. Remember, in those days they were not cruise ships. They were called passenger liners and they were primarily used to carry people from point to point. They were not used simply as floating casinos. I remember the *Oriana*, the

Arcadia, the *Canberra*, the great P&O passenger liners of that time.

I'll never forget arriving in Fiji in 1969 from Honolulu, when a band played at the dock one of the most stirring British tunes I've ever heard—quite an experience for me, a kid from the Bronx, to see that band of Fijians playing to the arrival of the ship. I spent many years in the Fiji Islands, collecting medicinal plants, living in villages, working with folk healers, mainly women, who told me their herbal healing secrets, and the ships brought me to them and brought me back from them to Hawaii where I was living at the time.

At this time I have my own ship, my own little sixty-foot ship called *Sea Talker*, and although I do not take it on grand voyages across large open seas, mainly sailing on it in San Francisco Bay, it brings me back to those early days of dreaming the big dreams on the West Side Highway of New York.

EIGHT

SLUM DIALECT

HOW I LEARNED TO SPEAK IS VERY INTRIGUING, GIVEN THAT
I am an immigrant's son. My father emigrated from Russia
when he was seven years old and he had a slight accent but
not a very pronounced one. Having grown up in the tene-
ments of the Bronx, I had somewhat of a slum dialect until
I went to college. I remember entering Speech 101; I was
asked to give a speech. We were told to listen to record-
ings of Winston Churchill and Franklin Delano Roosevelt
as examples of two of the great speakers of the time. I was
ashamed to speak publicly. I had a private conference with
my speech teacher. He was a very nice man. He said to me,
"You have a wonderful speaking voice."

I said, "But I say 'dem' and 'doss' and 'dis' and 'dat.'"

He said, "Don't worry about that." He said, "Just speak and eventually that will be forgotten."

And that's how I learned to dare speak in front of groups, where I got the confidence to speak publicly.

That is how I learned to give speeches: through the confidence given to me by this wonderful speech teacher at Queens College.

I always had a good speaking voice. Going back to the first grade, I was made the announcer. Why? I was the only kid in my class with a blue suit. God bless my mother, she bought me a blue suit, white shirt, and tie. So the teacher said, "Because you have a suit, you're going to be the announcer." I'll never forget getting up in front of that audience. I loved the feeling of looking at all those kids staring at me. I guess you might say I was born to lead audiences.

NINE

How I Got into Radio

I CAN REMEMBER THE DAY I RECORDED MY FIRST DEMO TAPE
and sent it out to more than two hundred stations around
America. I went down to Command Productions in the
Industrial Center Building in Sausalito. The building in
which this production studio is housed, incidentally, was
part of the old Kaiser shipyards. They built the Liberty
ships for World War II. It's an area I've spent a lot of time
in, just musing or walking about the boats, the docks,
the gas dock, looking at the boats. Anyway, I was writing books on health, nutrition, herbs, and I was doing corporate consulting, but I knew there was something more,
something more that I wanted. In fact, you might say I was

desperate. I was fifty years old and I wanted more. Just, things weren't right.

All the years I had done book tours, these grueling ten-city tours, I was told by various people of the media, "You really ought to go into the radio business. You have a great voice."

I said, "How can I go into the radio business? That's like telling someone to become an astronaut who can't fly."

Nevertheless, necessity *is* the mother of invention. And so I created the name Savage Nation and I went to Command Productions. I'll never forget to this day, I opened the tape like this: "And now, direct from the towers above Manhattan, it's 'The Michael Savage Show.'" And then I had my wife, Janet, call in and my old friend Frank call in from this little room that he lived in in San Francisco, during my monologue, which was against Affirmative Action. I had them call in with sort of staged calls. "Frank, you're next up on the Savage Nation!" That kind of thing.

Well, I had gotten from a distant friend a list of all the radio stations in America that had talk shows. It was more than two hundred, I think, at the time. I made the tape and sent it out to more than two hundred radio stations in the United States.

Within a week five stations said, "Hey, you're pretty good. Give us a call."

One, I remember, was in Boston. I don't remember the

others but one was in my own backyard, and that was the largest talk radio station in San Francisco. They said to me, "How would you like to fill in?"

Well, of course, I wanted to fill in on the most powerful station in San Francisco, 50,000 watts. So I did—a midnight-to-five A.M. shift for a guy who had a show that was devoted to hating white people and pandering to the worst in human nature. I filled in and did a normal show—actually it was quite an interesting show, not inflammatory at all, in my opinion. I talked about the inequality of Affirmative Action and things of that nature.

Well, I received such hate calls from the left-wing listener base that I was shocked, in the sense that prior to this I had been the good herbalist, the good doctor who everyone liked. I never heard such hatred in my life. For five straight hours I sat there and took it, and answered the best I could. As I drove home at dawn on Highway 101 to our little rental house, I remember looking in my rearview mirror the entire way back, thinking I was being followed. The hatred of the left-wing had literally provoked a semi-paranoid reaction in me. When I got home and my family woke up, I said to my wife, "I will never do radio again. It is so filled with hate, I can't take it."

Well, when I woke up, later in the morning, ring, ring, ring. "Hi, this is the program director. You did great, would you like to fill in for him again?"

I said, "Never. I'll never do radio again."

So she said to me, "Well, uh, would you consider doing another show?"

I said, "Sure, what other show?"

Now, remember, the day part radio shows on the 50,000-watt talk flamethrower, heard from Canada to Mexico, were the stars of radio. And so I started filling in for the day part radio shows. I created a storm. I was the first conservative in the media in the psycho left-wing San Francisco area. There was nobody before me, and frankly, there's been no one since me who could shine my shoes. Everybody knows that.

So I did fill in for a few months and then they came to me again and said, "Look, we're starting another station and it's going to be more conservative. How would you like to be the key player?"

"Sure, let's do it."

And so I did and the rest is history. That's how I got into radio.

The moral of the story is, just do what you do best and try the best you can until the day you die, and eventually the train that you are riding will lead you where you belong.

TEN

Achievements

ONE OF THE STORIES IN THIS BOOK TELLS ABOUT A MAN ON an island in Majorca who had threatened my life when I was young. The gangster. Well, if you remember that story as you read, you'll see that, as I looked through his scrapbook, there he was with his two new Jaguars and a blonde on his arm, showing off his possessions. That was then. This is now. Today we are not allowed to show our possessions; we have to hide them. In those days a man worked as hard as he could to gain as much as he could. Sometimes doing good, sometimes doing bad, but he didn't hide what he had achieved. At this stage of my life I have many things I cannot talk about: cars, planes, boats; but you don't want to hear about it because no longer does success matter. Failure seems to be extolled. Poverty is extolled, not the honestly earned riches. It's a world turned upside down.

I began by thinking I would be a scientist. In fact, I still have the little antiquated brass microscope that I purchased when I was a high school teacher. Little did I know then that I would wind up behind the microphone.

ELEVEN

Boy in the Basement

It was a market, see, and I apprenticed in there to the leader of them all, my little father, Ben. From about the age of four or five until my seventeenth birthday, that's where I received my major training.

I knew each one of the men in the market. It was laid out just like a ship. A long corridor down the center with five or six stalls on each side. Here we have Murray, and next to him was Fartser—Charlie was right next to Murray. That was the stand I later occupied when I began to sell antiques.

I remember Charlie from his heyday of screwing women downstairs in the basement—(all the rag dresses he'd given them) those poor women he'd invite downstairs—and I'd be watching through a slit while I was cleaning bronzes down there.

See, I used to work down in the basement at the sink. My father gave me cyanide solution to clear the patina off bronzes. They used to kill men in San Quentin with cyanide solution, right? So my father's friends would come down and see this Dickensian little boy in the basement, me, cleaning bronzes with a toothbrush. Scraping it off with the acrid, deadly, cyanide solution, my eyes getting all irritated. They'd say, "Benny," to my father, "how can you do that? It's your own son." And he'd say, "Never mind, it's good for him, it's good for his soul, it's good for his character."

In a sense, he was right. My other world in later years, the good suburban world of green-carpeted security, gave me little to think about. But there, in that cold, dark, unheated basement of the market, I had time to think, to develop the introspection of a prisoner. Basements still do that to me; they encourage clear thinking. It must be the closeness to earth, to origins, the security of walls without windows, the exposed supporting beams, the ancestral memories of refuge in these elemental places.

I remember my father's story about czarist Russia, where a basement saved the life of Uncle Philip. Invading troops came through the village seeking pillage, food, and general mischief. The women clutched their children and hovered near the small dwellings. As the leader passed my grandmother on a large white stallion, he reached down and grabbed my father, then a boy of three or four, from his mother's arms. She began to shriek, but the officer had a lighter end in mind. He simply pranced his horse around the village for the delight of the startled boy. When it came to the menfolk, though, the invaders had different thoughts.

They entered the little house, demanding the women reveal the whereabouts of the men and boys, who they hoped to conscript into the Polish army. As Uncle Philip, then fourteen or fifteen, hid in the root cellar, which was entered through some floorboards hidden beneath a piece of furniture, the soldiers pounded their rifle butts on the floor, one smashing my grandmother's foot as he left in disgust.

So, as a young kid, I'd be down in the basement of the market cleaning bronzes with cyanide solution, lost in my boyhood thoughts. Every once in a while I'd see Charlie waltz by with some beat-up woman, and she would say in the dark, "Well, where are the dresses?" And he'd say, "Oh, they're in here." As he always had hundreds of rag dresses, he'd lead them into his cold, damp basement and say, "Go over and pick out what you want." They took a few rag dresses and Charlie took them.

Anyway, once I was down there cleaning, and Charlie came out from giving rags to this woman, and he was wiping off his pants with a handkerchief. At the time I didn't know what had gone on in there. So my father walked by, and he looked at Charlie, and Charlie looked at him, and he said to Charlie, "Whatsa matter, Charlie, you spit on yourself?" And Charlie, he just laughed, wiping off his pants.

I mean this was the kind of subterfuge that was going on underneath the floorboards of the market. So I knew Charlie from those days, when he was at the height of his womanizing, when he was chasing the dead wye over the rags in the basement, right up to when he was dying of cancer, fifteen, twenty years later, in those hot summer days, while he still held out.

The market was right next to Neiberg's Funeral Home; that was where I saw my first corpse. It was a hot summer, and I learned from the undertakers who used to hang around in my father's market that there were seasons for death, that when people had terminal illnesses they would rarely die in the spring, and hardly ever in the summer. People with terminal illnesses would wait out the summer and die in the fall. My father eventually died in the fall; he knew the folklore. He was expected to die at any time, and he chose October.

But I remember Charlie as a dying man. It was his last season at bat. There he'd be, in his little gray suit. He always dressed neatly because, after all, he was a woman's man, even if it was those poor, beat-up women. In his mind, he was still a woman's man. And he always used to talk to me about women, from the time when I was a little kid. He always used to say, "Hey Mickey, look at her *fartsa*. Oh Mickey, look at her *fartsa*." This went on for years. Anyway, this was his last season in the dugout. He was sitting back in his booth with his wife and her cheeks made up, big red lipstick, a real dummy. So he was sitting there, Charlie, in his last season, with a little gray suit and a tie, sitting there on a chair. He had terminal cancer and he was moaning, low, but I could hear it even as he spoke to me. The pain must have been frightening. There he is with his eyes closed and all of a sudden, he's looking through the slits to stare at a young Puerto Rican woman prancing through the market. "Oh, Mickey," he said. I followed, "What, Charlie?" He said, "I'd like to *schtup* her once more." So, you know, I fell for it. I said, "Oh, you mean you made it with her before, huh, Charlie?" And he said, "No, once more I'd like to *schtup* HER."

As we move down the line, we come to Monk. Monk

was a bohemian whose old lady was Frances; she was the woman that I really fixated on through my early years. Frances, she was the beatnik. They were the two old beatniks.

I mean, they were commie beatnik bastards. Monk wore a rope for a belt. And where the other men put giant padlocks on their wooden booths when they swung the boards up at night, Monk would tie a rope around, a little string around his stall, as if to laugh at everybody. Years afterwards, I learned that during the Sabbath a string was tied around the shtetl, or villages, of the Carpathian Mountains. Mere strings to keep intruders from violating the day of rest. So Monk would tie up his merchandise with string.

Monk was a drinker. He was the strongest one in the market, and he was totally nonviolent, totally against war. He was the only guy to talk to me realistically. Where he'd get mad at me, the other guys would play with me at this and that. What did I know? I'd say things like, "Monk, you got any guns?" I was six and into guns. You know, being around antiques and used things I never knew what was coming in next, and that's what made that life interesting. There was always hope that the next lot of junk might contain something that I wanted. So I'd say, "Hey, Monk, do you got any guns, any pistols, or anything like that? Rifles, you know—" "What do you need guns for," he'd ask. "Guns are for one thing only—killing. Don't be a monster! Go away! Don't talk to me about guns!" he'd say, his broad face scowling.

Anyway, I liked Monk. Now, Monk had reputedly been a very, very powerful man in his youth. Once in a while he'd get very drunk. Sometimes he'd drink an entire bottle in a day; he was one of those guys. He always kept a quart of whiskey under his stand, and he'd lift it up by its neck, straight up to the ceiling, and he'd go "Glug, glug, glug," you know, and then put it down, wipe his mouth, and then go "ahh," and everyone would move back.

You've got to picture him: He was broad more than tall, he wore an undershirt in winter—he dressed like a clown, he looked like Chaplin but broad and wide with a severe, fierce, Carpathian Mountains face.

And what did he sell? Now, Monk looked like he was selling garbage. See, my father, in the stand, had his merchandise built up, with bronze figures on the near shelves and large candelabra towards the rear reaching to the plaster-cracked ceiling, like a stairway to heaven. At the top were the most expensive things, as in Coney Island booths. My father sold on an old principle: cheap things up front and expensive things in the rear. See, that way he could get you for lunch money, at least. But Monk had his merchandise on a one-tier stand, and it was all mixed up.

There was no order to it. He didn't even try to lay it out. He would take a box of goods and spill it out on the table. Now, who would buy from Monk? A surprisingly large number of doctors, really; some important men. One of them happened to be the head of a major hospital. Years later, I learned that he was the chief of staff. The old chiseler would come down to the market on Saturdays, on his day off, and he would bargain with Monk, because Monk would play games with the world. He would take gold and silver and mix it in with tin just to watch the chiselers go through it for hours, through the small pieces of jewelry, like rats scratching at the earth, waiting to pull the gold from the midst of the junk. If Monk was in a bad mood, he might do anything. His customers might ask, "Hey, Monk—how much is this?" He'd look at the guy, knowing that the piece might be gold or silver, and if he was in the mood he might say, "Ten cents," just to see their reaction, just to see them shake. As they paid the dime for gold, Monk would draw his true payment—derision. On the other hand, an inexpensive piece of jewelry might be priced out of all proportions. "How much is this?"—"You can't buy it." Or, if a woman wanted a tin bracelet: "It's not for sale." He would do just crazy things. He didn't do this all the time; he did it selectively. Monk would break people's balls, just to show them the irrelevancy of what they were doing. He made a living at it; he didn't have to work very hard.

Monk's old lady was Frances, and she was beautiful. She was a beautiful English beatnik—tan, long hair down to her waist; and she was so different from the women that I grew up with that, naturally, I fell in love with her. She was gorgeous. She wore dungarees. I used to hear Charlie Fartser talk about Frances once in a while. The other men couldn't admit they liked her, right? Because socially, who was she? She wore pants, dirty pants. But they loved her. I mean, they were hot for her. She was the only real woman around. Charlie would say, "I bet you can smell those pants up here." You know, they'd talk about how dirty her pants were. But they really loved her; you could see it in their eyes.

Years later, when I was a young merchant myself, Monk got sick. After a heart attack, he shrank in size. It was frightening; he went to Bellevue and came out looking one-third the size—a skinny man with no power, in a wheelchair. He told Benny he wished he was dead.

Frances was always friendly with homosexual types who would work in the stand with her. And this is where I really got a feeling for music, by watching them across the center gangway, where the market was open on both sides. I'd sit behind my father's stand and watch these men listen to music, and enjoy it. They'd play classical music, and they would move to it while they were cleaning something, polishing some metal. You'd see the men genuinely moved by the music. No one was watching them, so they were really relating to it as though they were in their own house. That's where I was first able to see a man, or a human, moved by music.

The only other Frances tale occurred in the basement when I was about thirteen and wearing my hair combed back in the semi-ducktail. She came downstairs; I was very shy, and I was there cleaning the bronzes, and she says to me, "How come you want to look like a teddy boy? Why do you want to look like a teddy boy?" Now, I was also insecure, and I had been ridiculed by my father so much that I thought she meant a fag, by her "teddy boy." But she meant a hitter. She was actually telling me, "Why are you trying to look so masculine?" while I thought she was saying, "Why do you look so feminine?" That's how distorted I had gotten by that point. It took me five years to figure out what "teddy boy" meant. Five years to figure out that Frances wasn't calling me a fag.

Now we get to Ethel, white-haired Ethel with the big breasts or, as they called them, bosoms. In her case they were not really sex glands. They served one purpose only: to say, I am a maternal, warm woman. So anyhow, she had these huge breasts, which were worn under a drape, a green velvet drape. She had white hair, cute little woman. Everyone thought she was nice. My father knew otherwise. They'd fall for her nice act. She'd cry, she'd give you a little candy or cake that she'd made. She was always crying about her sick husband. She always had rum cake which appeared to have been just baked in the back of her small booth. And she always told you about her sick husband and leaned on you, as if to say, "My sick husband is who I work for." My father used to say, "Ethel, please, stop weepin' for Christ sakes." So she would try to bullshit my father, like if a customer would come in to see my father, she'd get jealous. She was the only one who dared to carry the same merchandise as my father. She'd buy from the same guy and carry a small stock of the same things. She was right next to him in the back part of the market. So they'd come in to see my father's chandeliers, and there was a board running across the top between his stand and hers; and she had the nerve to hang a few chandeliers across this joint beam. To a big buyer from South Carolina he might say, "Well, the last one's not mine, it's Ethel's. Ask Ethel." So in a sense there wasn't that much open begrudging; it was a market and communal in a sense. You couldn't say, "Don't shop."

But everyone was in competition. My father was supposedly the richest. That was the only way he could be there. Even among that motley band, he had to be the wealthiest. But it wasn't true. He only thought he was the richest, I'm quite sure. Anyway, Ethel called my father the human fly, because he used to walk on the beams, above the stalls near the ceiling where he kept things. He'd balance himself from board to board, a little trapeze act for the crew.

Ethel had a son who was supposedly a CPA, only he wasn't a CPA, he was a PA, he blew the C. He wasn't certified; in other words, he was a failed accountant. She used to call him "my boy." He was forty-seven, not married, and she'd say, "Danny, my boy, I wish he'd meet a nice girl." This went on for twenty years.

In the next stand was Gene. Now, thus far, I've been talking about Jews, till we get to Gene. Gene was Italian; Gino was actually his name. Gene was married to this woman, Helen, and my father named her Helen Throw Bean for some reason. I don't know why. And Helen Throw Boob. Helen was this big bimbo. But Gene and Helen were fifty, and she'd lost all her looks, but apparently they were gorgeous as young people. She was a sweet woman through all that big lipstick and the crazy eyes dressed up with mascara, crazy lipstick, and the weird dresses and the high heels—she was a sweet woman. They lived in a teeny little flat.

They always had dogs that they loved. When one dog died, they closed the market, they were so sick for weeks.

And she told me once, when I was about fifteen, she said, "That's my Gino back there." She said, "You don't know about Gino. Gino is my golden boy. When he was young he had long golden hair. He was such a handsome man; he was very beautiful." She said, "Gino was very rich when I met him." It was always like that, you know, rich and beautiful. Gino supposedly owned a couple of automobile agencies, Chrysler agencies, which he lost during the Great Depression.

Many of these men in fact were refugees both of the old country and of the Depression. They were double refugees. And the market in essence was to them a gold mine, because they would make a living without working for someone; they were still independent, which was the most important thing to them. They were all first generation. My father was born in Russia as was Monk—they were all immigrants. See, they all came from another market together. At first, they just sold rags and junk off pushcarts, that's how they met. I think my old man also began with a pushcart after his dry goods business failed, during the Depression. So, for them to have a fixed store was really something. This was their market; they were merchants. A Ship of Merchants. But remember what a merchant was to a man with a pushcart—it was the Promised Land. I used to hear stories about the old market. And the division of loyalty that I grew up on was between those from the old market who came into the new one (they were the nucleus) and the newcomers who didn't count for a nail. They were the ridiculed ones. Ethel was a new one. Johnny was a new one. The original band was Benny, Sol, Murray, Charlie, and Monk. And that was about it. The rest were newcomers and therefore not even worth the time of day. They all knew each other only thirty years in the new market, but that didn't matter. Those not from the original crew were considered worthless.

Then we had, coming up on the right—what the hell was his name?—the eighty-five-year-old guy built like a sixteen-year-old kid. The Iron Man. Leo. Leo sold mainly jewelry and had gray hair, and was renowned as a philanderer. His wife would work so that he could get dressed up as a dandy with white gloves, hat, cane, and walk up and down Second Avenue. He was just a dandy, that's all. I saw him in his later years. But he was always interested in girls. At my Bar Mitzvah, I remember him coming up to me, and saying, "Oh, Michael, who's that? Who's that woman? What's her name?" It was some giant bimbo. She was married to a gambler and she had no fingers, but Leo didn't see that she had no fingers. Actually, she had stump fingers, she was born that way. It was weird. I remember she had all stumps. I was thirteen years old, and I'm seeing this guy getting crazy about this giant woman with big breasts, but he didn't know she had no fingers. I wanted to say, "Hey, Leo, uh, that's uh, so and so, but she got no fingers. I mean, you know, don't get too crazy." Of course I didn't say it. I think he eventually found out, you know, over by the ice sculpture carved in the shape of a left ventricle. That would have best typified the life you were about to be initiated into, at that fantastic pageant.

Coming up on the left we hit Benny. Benny cannot be paraphrased or discussed in a few paragraphs, so we'll have to skip over him. We'll leave him there in the shop mounting lamps for a little while, and we'll move right on. We're almost sweeping back to the door, when we come to Johnny, Johnny La Crut. Johnny had the lowest status. He was illiterate. He was the Italian organ-grinder. Johnny looked like the kind of guy who would have a monkey in the street, an organ-grinder. Sol took him in in later years. Originally he used to mount lamps for Sol, and then eventually he got taken into the market as Sol's semi-partner. Eventually he quit, and just retired; he was the smartest one. In typical Italian fashion, he was the only one who retired. He put away enough money living in a one-room apartment for twelve dollars a month to quit with a stash.

So we have Johnny La Crut, and then his boss, Sol. Sol was Cigarette Sol. You never saw Sol for a second without a Pall Mall hanging out of his mouth, and he always had tobacco stuck on his lip; he was always going, "pff, pff, pff," always spitting a piece of tobacco out of his tough lip: "Hello, Michael, pff, pff, pff." Sol was a very nice man; he was married to Effie. He was the brother of Charlie Fartser, who died of cancer.

Sol and Charlie were brothers. And Molly Bloom was their brother. Molly was the brother who didn't do anything; he was the bum. He lived with Sol and Effie and the three children in one small apartment. The years would go on, and he never left the ghetto. Never. Molly Bloom, I learned later, was a character of James Joyce; a woman, the daughter of a major. But in this case, Molly Bloom was this Jewish ne'er-do-well who lived with the brother and the wife in a two-bedroom apartment on Allen Street.

Molly earned his living by, every once in a while, going to the sales where the men who were the principles in the market bought their merchandise. Molly would occasionally buy lesser merchandise and sell it out front. The stuff that Molly bought to sell was something that nobody else specialized in—used eyeglasses. Our market was one of the only places in America that I know of where used eyeglasses were trafficked in the open. On a typical Sunday outside 137 Ludlow Street, at the corner of Rivington, you might see Molly, with his face all red from the cold, with a few trays of eyeglasses bought at auction—a few dollars for several hundred pairs. They were bought at a subway auction, you know; stuff that people left on subways—unclaimed stuff. SO, there would be several hundred pairs of glasses, all jumbled up in boxes outside 137 Ludlow Street, and Molly would be selling them. Now, who would buy them but the poorest people, mainly the poor Jewish people who everyone has forgotten today. People say that every Jew is rich; after all, the Jews supposedly own the banks and the newspapers, so therefore there are no poor Jews. Of course I grew up around all poor Jews, but you're not supposed to mention that. We were all supposed to be striving, you know, to control the world banking system. But Molly didn't know about that, and he figured the next best thing to owning a newspaper or an oil industry was to sell used eyeglasses outside 137 Ludlow Street. So his customers were poor people, and they bought eyeglasses. They felt it was cheaper than going to an optometrist, a schmoptometrist, and getting a prescription, and having it ground, and spending forty dollars for glasses. They bought for fifty cents or a dollar. Now, they didn't buy any pair of glasses; naturally, they bought glasses which fit them. If they were nearsighted they needed glasses that came from a nearsighted person; if they were farsighted they needed glasses from a farsighted person, and so forth. So how did they figure out if the glasses would work? Very clever—they tried them on. And what did they do? They read. So Molly would have a few torn pieces of newspaper, such was the eye chart they tested their new powers of sight on. There would be a few old Jewish dailies, like the *Forward*, the *Daily News*, and the *Post*. I don't mean a full sheet of paper, but a shred from the corner of the sheet. So these shreds of paper were mixed in with the glasses, and you'd see these old people putting them on, reading, throwing the glasses off, on and off, on and off, till they found something; and then they'd bargain with Molly, who'd knock a dime or a nickel off of the glasses, and that's how Molly earned his living. To this moment I can vividly see Molly standing there outside in the cold, selling glasses, smiling when I came up to see him, his breath an airy cloud.

So that's how Molly made money once in a while. That's how he would support his alcoholic habit and puke on the floor in Sol's house, and they'd have to move him out once in a while to a hotel. And once in a while he'd accidentally expose himself a little to the daughter. When Sol bought a vacation house out on Long Island, they'd invite Molly out but he never went to this house. He never left the East Side, for any reason. He loved the ghetto; he had everything he needed there. He had his bar, Hammel & Korn. That's all he needed, the gin mill next to the synagogue.

Anyway, Sol saved his money and bought a small place out in Patchogue. After a day on a boat out on the water, we'd all barbecue at the house. It was so gorgeous. My father was there, my mother was there, everyone was there. We were so rested and happy. It was summertime. The reason I liked it was that, see, I never had a father to do anything with; he worked seven days a week.

The reason that I knew I had no father, it hit me when I was eleven, was when I went to a father-and-son Boy Scout dinner. I was the only boy at that Far Rockaway dinner without a father. So another kid's father saw me—I don't know why, he must've seen my face with schlumped shoulders; not slumped shoulders but *schlumped*, bent. I was so sad. It was the grayest day of my whole existence. I didn't understand. You know, when you're a kid you don't know why you're depressed; you just don't feel good, and you don't know why. I mean, I was eliminating the roast beef dinner, and here were all these lame fathers making speeches and bringing their sons up for awards. So anyway, this kid Aaronson's father took me in, but his father was a weakling. I mean, I wanted him to be tough and loud—I wanted *my* father to be there, to yell at everybody at the Boy Scout dinner.

Because that's what Benny would do, was yell. I remember once in a while Captain Queeg Benny would walk the deck on the "merchant ship." He'd get angry; he'd throw his weight around every once in a while, and yell at everybody, and then one after the other he'd put them down: "And you, you funkin' moron, and you, you this," and then he'd give the entire crew the yell, "If it wasn't for me, the lot of you would be in shit shape. Don't bullshit me; you're all a buncha morons." And there wouldn't be a peep; they'd all stop what they were doing and all be in fear and trepidation. Arrested as in a painting, fixed in time; this one polishing an urn, that one appraising a fragment of precious metal, another arranging or dusting—all fixed in time.

I remember one particular thing that happened between Benny and me. I was about ten or twelve and had decided it was time I learned to box. Being a small kid, I had always been pushed around and wanted to punch back. My uncle Nate happened to be close with a black fighter named Brown who was then training for the fight that would have given him a title shot. It was to take place in June, outdoors in Yankee Stadium, just before the heavyweight title fight.

Anyway, Nate called Brown and told him that his nephew wanted to learn to fight. It was arranged for me to meet the big black fighter at the Salem Crescent AC, up in Harlem.

We met and Brown slowly explained that I would be needing to bring a jockstrap, a pair of shorts, sneakers, and a towel. I remember feeling shy and embarrassed at the jockstrap part. Here I was, with an inferiority complex a mile wide, and only a kid—not yet trained in making my initial reactions, not feeling I even had a pair of balls, a real pair, a man's pair—and this big black man is telling me I'll need to protect these, in an easy matter-of-fact way. Already I grew in confidence.

Nate drove me home, back to Queens, and parted after some coffee with my father (his older brother, who he worshipped).

The next day I beamingly told my father all the details of my meeting with Brown, who he held in considerable esteem, being himself a heavy fan, every Friday night glued to the set. We were all around the table, father, sister, and mother; it seemed even our part-Chow, Skippy, was in on this proud moment. At last the skinny weakling would learn to fight. He had decided, and the world responded. It would help him learn to fly.

The little man responded in his typical Prussian-Russian way. Reasoning backwards, with heavy doses of scorn, he declared, "Boxing; it's not for you. What, you go to Harlem every few afternoons by train? Are you kidding? Some six-year-old black will haul off and bust your head with one good right."

That was it. I was finished before round one. Icarus, not reasonably talked from his foolishness bust, dashed instead to the rocks below—no glue, no feathers, no sun.

Brown, by the way, trained for that fight all winter and into the spring, only to splinter his forearm just weeks before the big day. He was finished for good. Those kinds of breaks never heal.

Even if they weren't afraid of the little tyrant, they would pretend, which was enough to satisfy him. They knew it was his psychodrama. But they respected him anyway. In this sense, they respected his life. They respected him enough to let him yell. No one else yelled at anyone, see? In *The Call of the Wild*, he would've been lead team dog. The other dogs would have stopped, listening to the chief dog when it barked. They may have been feigning obedience, but that was enough—because therefore he was the boss. You understand? They didn't really have to hear him. He wasn't the wealthiest merchant, but he brought most of the good customers into the market. There were big buyers who'd come in from the South and buy a thousand, fifteen hundred dollars' worth of bronze from my father on a Sunday. That was a lot of money in cash. They'd also buy from other people, but they came primarily to see Benny.

Now let me bring in a few minor characters. There was Murray, my dear uncle Murray, beloved Murray. He was a beautiful man. Murray had a few character traits that were odd. He'd always repeat jingles that he heard on TV; he'd sing them during the day while working: "To look sharp, and be on the ball, to be sharp . . ." and so forth. He would always be humming, but when he would hum, my father would yell out from behind his stand, "Hey, Murray, you're chirpin' pretty good over there. You musta knocked in a couple grand today." And that would be the litany they would start off with, then, "Ah, Benny, stop. Who can make as much as you do?" They would go on like that. They knew Benny's weakness was to think he made the most, so they probably all figured, let him think he makes the most. But Murray ended up with a lot more money. Murray never sold as much, but he didn't spend as much, either. He led a very low lifestyle. He owned a house, but they never ate in a restaurant; they hated restaurants and things like that. They went home and that was it. They went to the market like Chinese, for their life was at home; they lived for their home and for their children.

OK, we've completed the main course. We're going to hit a few of the subcharacters. There were a few hangers-on: Goldsand, Morass—oh, the hangers-on were at least as interesting as the main characters—and Louie, who eventually had a monkey who bit him . . .

Goldsand is my very favorite adopted grandfather. He was a hanger-on who collected tinfoil for some reason. God knows what he thought he'd do with the tinfoil when the crash came. He must have had a gigantic ball of tin-foil somewhere—how big could it have been?—after fifty years of pulling tinfoil from inside cigarette wrappers and rolling them in a ball.

Goldsand was still alive; collecting a disability pension from World War I. What happened to him, he got mustard-gassed in France. Not badly, however, and he collected all his life. He was smart. He lived in a room for twelve dol-lars a month until they jacked his rent up to thirty-five; that almost killed him. He lived in this room without heat and slept wrapped in newspaper. Wrapped his feet in newspaper and slept under a dozen blankets, rags. But he also bought a house. Where? The country. He was the only one who bought a Catskill country property, which is quite valuable today. I'd go there in the early spring when no one was there; he'd give me the key, for me to go open it alone. Then I knew I was a man. And I'd come back to the city and he'd say, "So—how was the countree?" and he'd look at me with that beauti-ful face; he'd look up and ask, "How was the countree?" He always wanted to know how the countree was.

Although Goldsand was seventy-two years old he wasn't worried. He had forty-six more years to live.

How did he know?

Four years before, some very alarming symptoms overtook him. He began to sweat heavily, had difficulty breathing, ran a fever, the works. Sure that the end was near, Goldsand visited with Shapiro, the "king" of old men on New York's Lower East Side. Shapiro, who was then ninety-eight years old, asked his ailing friend, "What's the matter? . . . you afraid you're going to die?" "Yes," offered the ailing Goldsand. "How many more years you want? Fifty? OK, so you got 'em. Fifty more years to live."

That was four years earlier. Now Goldsand had at least another forty-six years to go.

The illness?

Oh, that was cured . . . with a piece of crusty Italian bread.

Goldsand, while enjoying what he thought was one of his last meals, indulged himself in a piece of this crusty loaf, quite different from the usual rye and pumpernickel. As he swallowed, he felt something tear off in his throat and a slimy fluid oozing out. And that was it.

From then on he breathed easier. His countenance was restored. No fever. Nothing. Rudetsky, the doctor to these men, later speculated that a small bone had become lodged in the old man's throat. A cyst enveloped this bone and began to grow. This is what the high fever was about, white corpuscles fighting off the invading growth.

And then we have Morass. Morass was a famed
bum who used to come in and out of the cold to get the
warm heat of the market, but he had to pay. His payment would be ridicule. See, he'd come in and they'd
start with, "Hey, Morass, come on over here, I need a
cup of coffee, you'll go out to the galley for me." He'd
walk over—he shuffled over from side to side, with
his overcoat and his red, runny nose—and he'd say,
"My name isn't Morass. It's Morris." "Yeah, yeah sure,
Morass—oh, I mean, Morris—I mean Morass." "My
name isn't Morass, it's Morris." And the interesting
thing is: Did they say "More Ass" or "he is in a morass"
because he was a bum? Or did they just play games with
his name? Were they Shakespearean? I mean, did they
know that a bum was in a morass? Another act would
be this: "Hey, Charlie," my father would yell, "did you
hear, someone saw Morass sitting in the galley eating
beans and whipped cream?" And Morris would yell
out, "That's not true. I never eat whipped cream with
beans. No one eats whipped cream with beans." And
then Charlie would laugh; a laugh of ridicule would ring
out, and then he'd say, "It's true, Benny, I heard it from
so and so. You know, the guy who owns the dry goods
store on Rivington." "It's not true. I don't care what
the dry foods guy said. No one eats beans and whipped
cream." All right, now if it happened once, you could

accept it. But this was going on for ten years, the beans-and-whipped-cream version.

And then there was Louie, another side character—to me the most fascinating, the one I loved most. Louie had long hair down to his shoulders. Louie was skinny; he didn't eat. Louie was brilliant. Louie was a bum poet. He got a monkey, but he didn't get the kind of monkey that everyone else got. You know, most get squirrel monkeys, those skinny, pathetic, stupid monkeys with skinny tails. Louie got some gargantuan woolly monkey with sharp teeth. Woolly monkeys are built like bears. Anyway, Louie used to clean bronzes for my father, whistling while he worked in "the pit." No one knew Louie was smart. When Louie painted our house, he taught me geometry. I was doing geometry homework and Louie would help me with it. Louie also did tricks for me in the dining room of the house. He'd bend a nail; he showed me different gimmicks. He could take a nail and bend it, and he was the one that taught me. He warmed it with his hand; he didn't put it over the fire. He said you take the thing, you put your thumbs on it, and you just keep the pressure up as tight as you can, never stopping for an instant—the nail will bend because of the heat. He taught me the psychology of bending a nail rather than the physical stupidity of it.

Louie lived with some woman over in Greenpoint,

Brooklyn, and he spent every cent he made at the bar, at Hammel & Korn. He'd go right from my father's market. At dinner, my father would say, "Louie, why don't you go buy yourself a pair of shoes?" "I don't need shoes, I got a pair." And he'd go get loaded in Hammel & Korn; he'd buy everybody drinks, the whole bar. I mean, when he had money he bought everyone drinks, and he'd do nothing but play the jukebox, smoke a cigarette, drink, and tap his foot next to the jukebox, whistling.

Well, as time would have it, Louie's lust was tested. Louie acquired twenty thousand dollars. How? He was walking, drunk, stumbled into a car that had a fender that was ripped off, a rusty thing, and he tore his leg open. He got some Hebe ambulance chaser, a brilliant lawyer, who won him forty thousand. Louie got twenty of it. Guess what Louie did with his twenty grand? That's right, he spent it in six months at Hammel & Korn. He didn't change his apartment. He didn't buy a pair of shoes. He did not buy an overcoat. Instead he got three girlfriends from Harlem and moved them into his house, and every night he appeared at Hammel & Korn and bought everyone drinks, and put money in the jukebox. SO, with his money, nothing changed; he just had more of what he did. And after the money was gone—ah, wait a minute! He did buy a few things with some of it. You know what he bought? Bronzes

from my father. The bronzes that he cleaned in the basement with cyanide. He came into my father's market, and
he bought bronzes from the boss. "All right, Benny, how
much is that?" Whatever my father would say, Louie's
answer was—"I'll take it." He bought bronzes. And then of
course when his money ran out, he sold them back to my
father. My father didn't beat him on them; he bought them
back for about the same price, which is what he always did
because they were always increasing in value. But, there
was the cleaning man buying bronzes from his boss. Now,
of course, I bought a bronze from my father as a result of
that, I think. Because the first money I made, I spent on
bronzes from my father, to show him that that's what I
wanted; and the one bronze I still own is a copy of Rodin's
Thinker. It's a powerful signed bronze, done in 1880. Louie
collected twenty G's and went down the tube anyway. Last
I heard, he was alive, and had had a heart attack also; he
was living in Greenpoint, alone, with an empty cage.

Another subcharacter comes to mind; a simple guy.
It's the first time I learned about schizoids. This guy was
a doctor. He came to the market with Afghan hounds.
He was the complete Dr. Jekyll and Mr. Hyde. All I knew
him as was "Doc." OK, Doc would come in on occasion,
most of the time beautifully dressed, impeccable, with two
Afghan hounds. Just a very cultivated-looking gent. On

the other hand, the same man would occasionally come in rags, disheveled, needing a shave, looking half-crazed, snot coming from his nose, and nobody dared to say to him that he looked fucked-up. They'd kibbitz him a little. They'd say, "Hey, Doc," Doc this, and Doc that. I remember once I went up to him and said, "Hey, Doc," and my father pulled me aside and said, "You never call him that, you don't talk to him in the tone we do." I said, "Why? Everyone else does." He said, "Because he understands when we do, he wouldn't understand when you do." Anyway, he was an alcoholic, and the only man I ever saw go through a complete double personality.

Next door to the market was Neiberg's Funeral Home, where I went downstairs at the age of eleven to see my first corpse embalming, and watched the whole thing. Later, I wrote a beautiful poem about it, about the woman's guts, blood running out, mixing with the garbage of the city in the Narrows, somewhere, flowing, and mixing with the sea. Anyway, there was this old woman being embalmed down there. I was eleven, standing and looking at her bouncing like a piece of jelly on the embalmer's slab, and when I came upstairs, there must've been a different look on my face. It was a hot summer's day. I was standing outside the funeral parlor; my father came out of the market: "Hey, Michael, where were you, Michael?" He said, "Were you downstairs?" I said, "Ye-yes, I was." He said, "Did you see?" I said, "Yeah, they showed me a corpse." And he got very upset, more upset than mad, my father, and he said to me, "You shouldn't a seen that. You shouldn't have a seen that. You're too young, you're too young." Of course, he was deathly afraid of death.

Now, there was a beautiful little undertaker by the name of Barney. He was a chauffeur, always neat. He'd hang out in the market. But Barney was the only man who said to me later on in life, when he'd see a pretty woman go by, "I had my share." And I repeated this to my friend once, I was about sixteen; and you know, later on in life that guy said to me, "I hope that when I'm Barney's age I can look at a young girl go by and say, 'I had my share.'"

THE VERY EARLIEST MEMORY I HAVE OF THE MARKET IS OF being brought there at age three or four, perhaps five, maybe on a Sunday, with my sister Sheila, who is older than me by a few years, to sell our used comic books. For me it was a great escape from the Milk Police, my mother and her tenement lieutenants. My father taught us not to throw away old comic books. He told us, "If you want to make some money, take the books you bought for ten cents, put them in a neat stack, draw a line through the ten cents with a big black crayon, and mark them down so you can get five, six cents." And to us, this was simply a miracle. I mean, that you could get any money back for something you had used was incredible. Sure enough we tried it, and we were able to sell our joke books. So we'd go down on the weekends, and of course this is how we were broken in to the concept of merchandising. Very similarly, if you go to a Chinese grocery in San Francisco, you might still see a young child learning to count on the abacus from a grandmother or a grandfather, or learning how to give change. Training is very early. We didn't need *Sesame Street* to teach us how to add and how to subtract. We learned to add and subtract the minute we figured out that it had some value to us. If we paid ten pennies for something and could get five pennies for it, we knew we had five pennies more than the kid who threw the comic book in the garbage. SO, that's basically how you learn to add and subtract, and that's the basic value of mathematics. We didn't need any "New Math," no old math; it was called simple arithmetic.

The apprenticeship continued. I would go in with my father on a weekend, usually a Sunday. I remember in the early years before things went bad for my father—and I don't mean businesswise, I mean with my brother sick and all, the one who was eventually hospitalized in a mental institution—before things really got on him and he had a nervous breakdown when he was about thirty-five. I remember he was joyful on Sundays, which I would spend with him. There were a lot of games we used to play in the market. Games like these:

Physically the market was laid out so that there were approximately one, two, three, four, five different-sized stands on the left side of the market as you faced the front to rear, and five on the right, with steps at the rear going downstairs to the basement. And each stand had wooden doors that swung down and up, which were locked at the end of the day. On a typical Sunday, the market was filled with people. It was something to behold, like Coney Island or maybe Ripley's Believe It or Not! Museum. It was jammed with sightseers, real buyers, no buyers, bums in and out of the cold, natal hippies; it was just fantastic, the beautiful hum of people on a Sunday, out spending time and money. And, you know, it was busy, just busy—it would be like a stage; the show opened, the crowds came in, and by three or four o'clock it was packed. Sometimes you could hardly walk through the crowd. And there was a beautiful feeling of prosperity in the air. To me it didn't matter, money or not. Obviously commerce was at the base of it all. But it was the buzz, the buzz we used to hear, that really turned me on.

So the crowd would be out on the main gangway of the

Ship of Merchants, walking. There'd be someone gobbling the peanuts and dropping the shells on the wooden deck, eating and gobbling and dropping, eating and gobbling and dropping. And Benny didn't just stand there and take it. He wanted to get even a little. So, naturally, there evolved a whole array of pranks that were played on the customers. They were all gentle tricks. The one I liked best as a young kid was the least complicated: You simply squatted down behind your stand, where you couldn't be seen. There was always a forest of bronze candelabra between you and the people, so they couldn't see you—not with all the lights bouncing off the shining bronze. They could only see the bronzes and the paintings and the clocks. So we'd squat down, my father and I, and he'd have a water gun, and we'd squirt through the bronzes and water a person. Now, of course, the beauty was not just squirting, but to observe the human reaction to being surprised. It was so primitive; we were two primeval hunters attacking invaders and watching their reaction as they were stung with our poison darts. The typical reaction would be: "Hey!" as the victim glanced up. It was very logical; they're not stupid. The man gets wet inside a market, he figures the ceiling is leaking. He doesn't assume there is a man squatting down behind his merchandise, squirting him with a water gun. So he looks up at the ceiling. And he starts to complain.

He says, "Hey, mister," to somebody behind a stand. "Hey, mister, your skylight is leaking" meant that the guy had been squirted by Benny and Michael behind the bronzes. And there was a standard response to that: "Nah, I'm telling ya," they'd say, "there's nothing—the skylight is not leaking, we just had it fixed." "Look, I'm, not crazy," the guy would argue, "I'm telling ya, I got wet. The skylight is leaking." "Naahh, the skylight's not leaking, you oughta go have your head examined better. There's no water comin' in." And this way they'd steam up the customer till he was almost at the point of socking somebody, and then they'd grudgingly admit, "Well, maybe the skylight is leaking a little, we'll have it checked." And that would disarm the guy. So that was one of our gimmicks.

Now that you must appreciate, the beauty of being four years old, or five, and squirting another adult with the complexity of your father—I mean, he even thought it up—can you *picture* the beauty of it? Great. I'm glad you can. Because as I got older, there were still other tricks. The simplest is one I'm sure you've seen elsewhere, but to a child who had never seen it, it was magnificent. What was the gimmick? You'd solder a quarter really well onto a nail. And you'd hammer the quarter into the wooden countertop, in an out-of-the-way place, kind of away from your view. And then on a busy day you'd make believe that you were occupied elsewhere, and you'd wait to see who would try to steal the quarter. It was a beautiful thing to see the hand reach out, the "thief" waiting for you not to look. As he'd grab the quarter and try to pull it away, it would stick to the counter, and the look on his face—the look of how he was caught; his hand caught in a bear trap.

Another of our games was the tapping trick, which carried me from the age of six to about thirteen, fourteen. This must have been developed in a carnival somewhere, because it was somewhat of a barker's cane that was used, although if you didn't have a cane, a yardstick could substitute, or even a small stick. It was simple. Here was how we'd set it up: A man would be at my father's counter bargaining with him, or at someone else's counter, and you'd go up behind in the crowd. Of course, you wouldn't give away your trick by looking down; it had been perfected. You'd place the cane just above his toes, over his shoes. And just as he'd reach in his pocket to pull out a coin, to pay for merchandise, you'd give him a good tap right on the toe just as the coins came out. That's it. The guy was finished. He'd look down. You'd pull the cane away and he'd start looking down. He'd search the floor; he was sure he'd dropped the coin because it hit his foot. He'd start in, he'd say, "Look, mister, I dropped a coin," and then of course the other guy would say, "You didn't drop nothin'.

I'm tellin' ya, ya didn't drop. Stop botherin' me, you're making it up." And this guy would search and search and he wouldn't go away; for fifteen minutes he'd be looking on the floor for a coin that never existed.

Now, if that doesn't turn you on, we had a better method. Actually, the tapping game was fantastic, because you'd find people have very different sensitivities. I mean, there were times when I was *hitting* people on the feet with a yardstick—you'd start with your tap light; no response. You'd tap a little again; no response. Again, again; no response! Till you're actually pounding on the guy's foot with a stick. No response. To vitalize the sensitivities of these dull-footed individuals, another variety of the tapping game was originated. This was the jingling game. You would simply take a coin and drill a hole in it. Then you'd cut rubber bands and tie them together so they made a string, and you'd tie the rubber band string through the hole in the coin, and you'd wrap one end around your finger. And then while the man dug for a coin in his pocket, as he was paying, you would throw the coin in your hand out onto the wooden floor so it jingled, and it would bounce right back, really fast, faster than the eye, almost, and the man would look down, right? He was sure he dropped the coin. And those guys were the worst. When you pulled that trick, that was the final one, because you would get them looking for an hour. They would search through the dust and the grime underneath the counter for the coin they were sure they dropped; a coin they would never find.

A few other details come to me regarding the dear old market. In particular, I remember, in the back of the store, there were two of those dimwitted signs bearing particularly cute American phrases. One was to the effect, "We grow up too soon old and too late smart." It took me years to figure that out; by the time I'd figured it out, it was too late to do anything about it, I was too old. And the other one was from the class of sayings, like, "Old golfers don't die, they just lose their balls." But this one in particular struck me every day as I went to the bathroom downstairs in that dingy, dark, depressing, stinking bathroom that I was afraid to pee in. It stank, it had a dim 20-watt yellow electric bulb, it was cold. And inside this horrible bathroom, atop this stinking urinal, inside this freezing, cold Dickensian basement craphouse, there was one of those "old golfers lose their balls" signs, and this one said in pseudo-Yiddish script, "Please piss in the bowl." Of course it took me years to understand, (a) that it wasn't in Yiddish, and (b) what it said, that it really just said, "Please piss in the bowl." For years, I thought it was some kind of religious sign to do with peeing; you know, from the Old World, like from the Torah. Well, what can a kid know? SO, it took me years to figure that one out.

Now I'm jumping ahead to years later. My father has had his first heart attack and it's a great trauma to the family, because he was this great strong man, yelling, telling everybody what to do and he was usually right. Finally, the patriarch of the family was laying under oxygen. Number One Son, ripped from college, has to take over getting the family income. So I would open up my father's antiques market every morning, and try to do a little business. And I didn't do too badly, I thought; I brought home a few—five, six hundred—bucks a week, gross income; who knows what it netted? Nevertheless, there was a little cash flow coming into the house. You guessed it. It wasn't good enough for the old man. Under oxygen, he gets my report: "How's business?"—"Not bad. Moe came in, he took his lamps." "What: What lamps? Don't let any of those sons-abitches bullshit you. They'll come in and they'll tell you, 'how's Benny,' and this and that, and they'll look to rob a pair of candelabra on ya that cost me seven fifty." All right, that's not good enough. He's laying under oxygen there, a week in the tent, he remembers, he gets a bug in his head. In front of the antiques, he sold old clothes—to always be safe; he had it all figured out. In front he sold used clothes, a rusty razor blade, an old knife, an old fork that he bought at an auction. He took in ten cents, fifteen. He always said it made lunch money; if the antiques didn't sell, he'd

make money from the junk in the front. As you progressed
back, the merchandise became more expensive till finally
at the top tier was the expensive stuff. So under oxygen
he remembered his lot of clothes. He asked me, "How are
the clothes going?" Who remembered clothes? To me it
was a bunch of rags. We'd throw the boxes out and let the
bums go through it. He said, "What about the sweater?" I
said, "What sweater?"—"The ski sweater, the good black
sweater, the Austrian sweater." "I don't know about no
sweater," I said. "I sold it to someone for about two bits,
twenty-five." That did it. In his oxygen, they almost had to
come in and give him a sedative. That his stupid son running the family show sold a sweater worth at least three
dollars for a quarter. This was all that was on his mind.

Now, Benny's beautiful paranoia was a reflection of his
image of the world, which was based largely on his many
years working among the cream of society of the Lower
East Side of New York. Take the way he entered his stand
in the market. He backed into it. I didn't know from backing in, walking in forwards, whether to go it sideways.
There was a little corridor entering his booth, and then in
front was the merchandise. He'd always warn me, "You'll
always walk in backwards. Never take your eyes off them.
You take your eyes off them for a second, they'll hit ya like
a hawk." He'd say, "They'll look ya right in the eye, they'll

talk to ya, and they'd wait for ya to blink, and the minute ya blink or ya sneeze, boom! Ya lost somethin' and you'd never know it." So, as you would guess, he figured out in the oxygen tent that someone clipped an Austrian ski sweater from me because I failed to back into the stand; that is, I didn't walk in backwards at work. At college you had to do that a great deal, walk backwards into your seat. Can you imagine that? It's pretty crazy. What a reality. I mean, how was I supposed to have known to walk in backwards? But in his mind, he probably thought professors backed slowly into their rooms, never taking their eyes off the students for fear that some philosophical wizard would steal a thought, you know what I mean?

Another guy pops to mind. This was the freak, the one-titted man. His name was Harry the Freak. Harry started out as a freak in Coney Island. Just a regular barnyard freak. And his big attraction was that he had one tit. Big deal. He billed himself as "Half Man–Half Woman." As years went on, he became fairly well off. He became a capitalist freak, and he opened up his own sideshow in Coney Island. He employed and exploited his freak brothers and sisters, the microcephalics, the macrocephalics, the midgets, you know, the standard dwarf that would say a little thing with his voice and scare the kids, "blah, blah, blah," you know. And the bearded lady, too. But Harry's game was running the freak show, and he made a lot of money—and where would he spend it? This distorted, twisted man would buy beautiful antiques; that was his counterbalance. And he'd spend virtually all his money on such merchandise. He lived in Long Beach, in a little *Godfather*-like house. It was strange. From the outside it was a regular house in Long Beach. You'd knock on the door—I remember I went a few times with my father to make deliveries of, oh, a bronze figure of something, or a grandfather clock—and the door would open, but never all the way, only just a crack through which you would come in sideways, schlepping the thing in with you. And there it was: from floor to wall to ceiling and back again, with no apparent order, merely a storage house of antiques. No order, no rhyme, no reason to the display; as he got them, he dragged them in, found a place for them, and stuck them there on the floor, maybe moving a few things around. And this was the world he lived in. He treated his antiques just as if they were mere objects of art. So in a sense he had a purer vision of what these things were. He didn't worship them, give them a pedestal or a special place; he merely liked associating with them, and treated them as such, as mere objects. SO you might say that Harry the Freak was really an antiques chauvinist.

In the beginning, the 1940s, the men at the market earned their living primarily by buying merchandise that had been left in the subways, unclaimed merchandise, unclaimed steamer trunks and the like. I was told that in those days, if a trunk was unclaimed it was sealed at the wharf and then put up at auction, unopened. Which means in the good old days of the thirties and forties, you used to bid on the trunk according to what the trunk looked like in value on the outside. If it was an expensive leather with brass fittings, you bid accordingly. You could never tell what was going to be inside. But the men liked playing the game. It was interesting to them because it was taking a chance. They'd bid maybe seven dollars for a good trunk; four or five dollars for a poor-looking one. And they'd buy six, seven, eight trunks at auction, take a little truck, and haul them into the market, usually late at night. As they proceeded to open the trunks up, everyone who went to the auction, they'd have a kind of free-for-all, comparing who did better in the game of chance.

One trunk story in particular sticks in my mind. One trunk had belonged to a nun. They could tell it was a nun's trunk because of the photographs inside. They had also found her habits in there—a few old nun's habits and articles indicating she was also a nurse.

As they were rummaging through, looking for a few valuable candlesticks or whatnot to put up for sale and get back their seven bucks profit, they found a strange

object at the bottom wrapped up in muslin. Being inquis-
itive sorts, they proceeded to unfurl the muslin package.
What would be at the heart of this onion-like skin but
an embryo. A human embryo, all wrapped up neatly in a
nun's trunk.

TWELVE

HEGIRA FROM NEW YORK

My first hegira from New York was a bus ride to Miami.

The dining highlights I recall were the chicken bones in a greasy bag, thrown under the seat by an old lady going to her retirement; and chicken again, this time the "Southern Fried" variety at a bus rest-stop in the middle of an Atlanta winter night. I always loved fried chicken as a boy, and this was really going to be a treat. To gorge on greasy chicken thighs and breasts in the heart of Dixie, where I had heard they had first perfected the recipe.

The only factor limiting my enthusiasm was the time. I was asleep like Ratso Rizzo (Dustin Hoffman's grizzled drifter in *Midnight Cowboy*) on his death ride, sweaty and in a fit of sorts, when the jouncing Greyhound abruptly stopped. The lights were flashed on. "Rest Stop, everybody out," shouted the bus driver, and he came down the aisle prodding each and every one of us, even the old chicken-bone lady, reminding me of the cartoon cop of the past who cracks his billy across the soles of the sleeping park bum.

Maybe he got a kickback from the rest-stop owner, I really don't know, but everyone on that bus was hounded into that eatery, the doors to our carriage locked; there was no escaping it. I would have Southern fried chicken, even though I was slightly nauseous beneath that three A.M. Georgian night sky with stars as sharp as fractured mollusks in a barrel.

It was OK, that's all. Too crusty, too greasy. Of course, today I know it was probably cooked in lard, and that the saturated fat would account for my early death had I kept on with my dietary ignorance. But the slight case of indigestion I nursed all the way to Jacksonville gave me that slight something to think about, which oh so softly pushed me into the arms of Morpheus.

Miami

In those days (c. 1958), you could get a full breakfast for thirty-nine cents. Two sunny-side-up eggs, fried in butter, one slice of grease-ridden ham, two slices of white toast suffocated in butter, coffee, and juice.

I loved every bite, but have never again eaten anything like that. Now it's one healthful (and bland) dirge after another. But I'm still alive, which is an achievement in this world. Balancing your wants against your needs without becoming homicidal or suicidal is success, though I will admit to approaching both states several times along the road.

Kerouac's *On the Road* had just surfaced at Queens College. Harold, the older, fat boy in the crowd, smilingly fished it from his tentlike trench coat one rainy autumn day in Flushing. He told us younger guys, milling around between classes, that the book portrayed a wild car ride across America. Free sex, saxophones, and drugs on every page.

As they say today, it was a real "page-turner." My first, really—unless you count that book I read when I was about eight about some guy who flew a seaplane into Arctic lakes, saving Eskimos and trappers.

Kerouac's odyssey was not about saving others; he was

on his own road of salvation, seeking drama through thrills, not yet knowing that peace within came only when the trips were over and you could sit on a balmy pier watching the gulls while thinking about where you had been and what you thought you were doing there.

Now, it is true that Tolstoy died in his eighties, covered with snow on a train station bench after setting off on one more journey. And that there is something defeatist about saying you're through traveling while still young and healthy.

This attitude is true sacrilege in a nation obsessed with motion. But, like Kerouac, America too will learn her limits and I hope it's before we burn out in an old armchair in front of a television, drunk and drugged, watching another one of our endless foreign "peace" missions.

But Harold's book was just the kick I needed to unchain myself (so I thought!) from clan and caste. So during midsemester break, it was my first bus trip to Miami, followed in later seasons by a wild nonstop car ride, eight of us packed into a fast hemi-Dodge, and later still, an army surplus DC-3 that taxied on a tail-wheel from Newark. Tilted at 45 degrees, you felt like Buck Rogers about to take off on a space adventure. Until the stewardess, not yet a "flight attendant," distributed those box lunches that smelled of cardboard.

Other than being robbed in a fleabag hotel by a midget bellhop, who pulled some kind of trick on me by making my bankroll of eighty dollars disappear from the hotel's safety box, nothing much exciting happened down there.

It is true I got my money back by causing a bad scene, provoking seedy Orson Welles types to slowly close in on me in a circle, only being saved at the last minute by the Dade County blue boys. They came, mind you, because the midget had called them in an attempt to intimidate this Yankee into backing off on his crazy demands. But when the six cops arrived, as I say, I was surrounded by an assortment of perfectly fine carnival geeks, and the *midget* suddenly discovered that my money was somehow still in that steel box.

Must have fallen down in back somewhere, that's all.

Charged with pulling victory from what would have been fiscal disaster on my first solo flight from the nest, I took my friends to dinner.

And I don't remember the meal, and that's all I've got to say about eating in Miami.

THIRTEEN

AN AMERICAN GANGSTER IN SPAIN

MAJORCA

THE FIRST RESPECTABLE MIDDLE CLASS "BUM" I MET WAS A
soon to be high school principal from Brooklyn who
smoked "dope," danced the mambo like a Cuban, "had"
lots of women, and walked with a minstrel smile at all
times. Very dark-skinned for a Caucasian, and with thick
lips and curly hair, he was the Hebraic male version of
Abraham's wife, Sarah, said to be comely and black.

Anyway, Donny had just come back from a very far-away place, where the wine, women, and *danzóns* were said to flow as freely as in Impressionist Paris days. I, right then, decided to go there. That summer, or as soon as I could afford it, I'd go to Spain and get over to Majorca.

It was a converted troop ship, the MV *Waterman*, that carried my friend Marty and me on our pilgrimage to Donny's paradise island. Two years it took me to save up for that trip. When we first escaped our moorings with deep foghorn vibrations not matched by today's jet whine, all of my past seemed to slip beneath my feet.

This was going somewhere!

The last person in my family to ride a ship was my father on his immigrant journey to America. Turning around on the stern, drunk with Marty and a couple of hundred other budget-minded travelers, and feeling New York's West Side recede as in a dream, I knew I'd cut the umbilical cord for good.

Out to sea and seated for my first meal, I knew the next ten days would be bad news for food. Cheap German food served by surly waiters not older than you are does not make for an appetizing prospect.

So I took to sneaking into the first-class lounge each night and heaping the tasty little sandwiches into my raincoat. Those ham and other cold cut sandwiches beat the sauerkraut and potato soups served in our class, but also served to make me impotent just when I met my first international beauty.

She was coveted by all the boys. Tall and pale, rarely smiling, Karen was the daughter of some World Bank executive. Brought up in Swiss and English boarding schools, she was the dream of every working-class, would-be poet on that tub.

The first guy to win her attention was Andrew, a tall ugly screwball who imitated the French existentialists by throwing potato salad at ship lecturers.

After five days of this brilliant joker, we took up together. Slowly at first, she telling me she liked me because of the way I walked. Something about my feet hitting the ground in a positive, assertive way, she told me in a Paris hotel room weeks later.

It was all innocent hugging and kissing on the *Waterman* for us. I pretended to "respect" her too much to proceed, but in reality I couldn't get excited in the right part of my body.

My heart would pound, my thoughts would swirl, my weight-lifted arms would nearly crush her breathless, but the right thing was not being transmitted below my waist.

Years later, I would learn this bout of "impotence" was directly related to the ham sandwiches I was filching from the first-class lounge! Not as a result of guilt for my transgressions, but due to the sodium nitrates and nitrites the ham was laced with. While these preservatives killed off would-be bacterial colonizers, they also killed a man's ability where desire was not lacking.

In sufficient amounts, the nitrates are used to quiet libido. It is rumored that in the military they gave this stuff, in the potassium form, to the boys—called it "saltpeter."

Now, who would have guessed that a good old ham sandwich, or other preserved meats—bologna, sausage, hot dogs—will ruin whatever good fortune may bring your way during your travels. But should you be eating some of these preserved meats three times a day, while also lacking phospholipids necessary for sperm production, a simple dietary adjustment could render years of psychoanalysis into the redundant torture that it is.*

You've got to be careful when traveling. To know what to eat and what to avoid must not become a full-time obsession, but you don't want to end up in a garret with the bells of Notre Dame cathedral tolling, white high heels askew on the floor next to a hastily opened lady's suitcase, lying there in a sweat trying to explain away your failure.

---

* The nitrates and nitrites are also carcinogenic and associated with Alzheimer's disease.

Karen *was* understanding. And she did come all the way from London to be with me, after all. But not knowing about the nitrate family and their vicious habits once inside the human, we began to blame *ourselves* for this unignitable passion.

As the days went by and my diet of good French food drove away the German ham and white bread, I returned to that state of vigor common to twenty-year-olds. The romance, once inflamed, burned on for a week or two in a magical Paris I've never, ever since known.

Then, the long-legged pale beauty went north, I went south, not to meet again except by chance in the mouth of a London Underground tube years later.

About to descend the steps with my wife of two weeks, Karen was ascending, arguing with a decadent-looking longhair. Our faces met. We were startled to bump into each other so unexpectedly. I looked healthier than I had during those days in Paris, fuller of myself, stronger in my step, while she was emaciated, almost pimply.

We said a few words, quickly parted, and never saw each other again.

But on that first "big trip to Europe," I did get to Donny's fabled Majorca.

The food was so unlike New York, the land and the people somehow so much more alive, that I stayed on, missing the next semester to sample all that the poets had promised.

PALMA, 1966

CHRISTMAS DAY IN SHATZY'S BAR. I'D BEEN THERE SINCE the summer. I was a regular among the expatriates, mainly English retirees living on pensions, playing at art.

The eggy taste of *Advocaat*, a creamy yellow alcoholic slammer, was fashionable in the Mediterranean port bar. One thing I liked about those English writers, they just drank, without a wink, devoid of "cute" American names for their addiction.

(In Alabama, I once learned the craziest name for a drink: "Slow Screw Against the Wall"—vodka and 7Up. These were glowingly taught to me by a group of very sweet Alabamian college girls, welcoming me to the Huntsville airport for a lecture I was giving the next day.)

So, again, another season of too much alcohol (and of the wrong kind), and tasty but suicidal food. Years would pass before I learned that diet was somehow related to my mood and performance, and which to prescribe and pro-scribe for myself and others.

Shatzy, wiry and friendly, took a liking to me. One rainy and windy afternoon, after I had motor-scootered in the 7 kilos from Arenal, a beach town where I had an apartment, he told me to get off the island.

"Kid," he whispered, his eyes screwed up behind a smoke cloud, "get out of here, off this island, fast." I was shocked. Thought the crowd liked me. "Why, what do you mean?" "Look, you're young. All they want from you," he said, lifting a shoulder in the general direction of the others in that smoky bivouac, "is your money and your woman."

Stunned, I looked around that tank full of human fish. Were these angels and guppies really piranhas beneath deceptive markings?

Over there, at the end of the mahogany counter, his legs twisted over one another like a rubber man, an Ichabod Crane—a drunken grin radiating from his fixed jaw— was an English "nature" poet, little known beyond that grave circle.

It could not be him. He was too drunk and too kind, all the time. Collapsed on the bench along the right wall after cursing out some old lady who dared say "Merry Christmas, Mike," was a loud-mouthed Irish novelist whose latest had just appeared as a film. His pretty, kindly wife and their three-month babe were like a quiet painting next to him, she nursing the infant while her husband slept off his latest drunk.

Definitely not them. Too honest.

Well, the Americans in the bar, sure. Highly suspect, and therefore, no threat.

That left only Max. The ex–mob boss on the run who I thought had befriended me.

Ya! The more I thought about him the more I began to believe Shatzy.

"Listen. I know this doesn't seem real to you but, I tell you, you're in danger."

My eyebrows arched and he ordered a free *Advocaat* for me.

Max Roachman first attracted my attention because of his heavy New York accent. As I thought about it, it was Carla who was first drawn to him! I remember her saying with that tee-hee little giggle of hers, "You remind me of my father . . ."

"Oh, that little . . ."

He had us up to his place after that first night. His Spanish maid, a quiet older lady, cooked an authentic spread.

Brought over by successive waves of colonizers—the Arabs, Berbers, and Moors—fruits are so prevalent that they accompany most courses.

We began with local wine soaked in sangria, the fruits coming from Maxie's own trees. Standing on the stone terrace and eyes wandering up to Arenal Palace, I felt very much at home.

His lousy record player was turning *The Memory Years: 1925–1950*, as this stocky old tough spluttered on about his wild days.

Well, what harm would it do for me to drink his wine and eat his food? (My money and my woman!)

Chomping on my first boar, with potatoes and artichokes, I listened as the old guy reminisced.

He sees me smirking and jumps up. "Here, you don't believe me," and he rummages through some old photo albums, his maid looking on from the archway with a sad, knowing look.

Headline: KING OF THE HOBOS HAS PENNY RAIL PASS—TRAVELS ONLY 1ST CLASS. He is shaking hands with railroad officials.

Next: Two dark-haired sisters, one on each side of Max in a nightclub: "Took 'em both home for four days." Next: Max smiling in an auto showroom, shaking hands with a happy salesman who just sold him a Jaguar MK V *and* a Jaguar XK 120.

"A good time, kid, but my wife got mad when I didn't come back home for nine months."

We eat the paella Valenciana. All the seafood fresh from then-clean bays.

The phono spins off speed.

Over flan and coffee, he worked himself up to his true

confession. A small news article tells us about his first murders: two boys in a train yard.

Then, with a flourish, a letter from then New York mayor Bob Wagner, inquiring about Max's recent operation.

"I got friends, kid." The books, records, suits, coats, shoes (I sneak a peek into his closets on the way to the bathroom), all "from friends," some items delivered by visiting U.S. warships, if we are to believe this old crook.

"What happened? I can't go back. That's all. Kid, it's all over now, all over." (*The Memory Years* spinning off speed.) "Too much, kid. I was too young."

But this story came to a bad end, though not quite at that dinner party. I must have known that good old Maxie was fiddling with my girl because, days later, I decided to get past his housemaid and snoop around his flat. To find "material" for a story I decided to write about him.

Against her pleading will and nonbelieving eyes, I talked my way around her objections, saying that Max had given me permission to reread his scrapbook. I don't remember what I found, but I did invade the man's privacy and was nearly killed as a result.

Served me right, I suppose, but I guess Max had a shred of compassion left inside somewhere. Days after Shatzy gave me that warning to get off the island, I would see Max everywhere I went. Sitting in a restaurant or a café, or wherever I would be, there Max would be. Staring at me, or visibly pointing me out to some of the notorious Guardia Civil, who we had heard would kill for fifty dollars, the going fee.

That was it. I got the message. Shatzy was right. I left. Oh, by the way. I almost forgot to mention what kept him imprisoned in his little bar. He told me this on the day he warned me to leave and start a life for myself while I was still young.

"Me, I can't go anywhere," he told me, his melancholic puppy eyes wet with emotion and smoke.

"It was my big night. I was lead dancer in London's biggest ballet. The performance was on. It was my call, I froze in the wings . . . I was finished. Here I am, forever."

FOURTEEN

SETTING A PEANUT
MAN ON FIRE

COMING OF AGE, 1952

As a kid Schwartz was a normal, if somewhat malicious, mischievous type.

He once set a "Planters Peanut" man on fire, on Broadway.

It was a holiday break, cold but not yet freezing so probably around Thanksgiving. We had taken the long subway ride in from Jamaica and were absorbing all the action that Times Square had to offer to two twelve-year-olds in from the green-carpeted world of the suburbs.

Coming out of the tube onto Forty-second Street, there was a mini playland of machines right next to the porno shop. In those days, porn was illegal so this place was put up as an "art" shop. Selling mainly B&W glossies of bimbos down on their luck—to us each a beauty, a masturbatory beauty, good for many hours of holiday fun.

Invariably the perverts who liked young boys stalked this recreational area. They would watch us, Schwartz the tall kid and me the pip-squeak. He would have the "nerve" to leaf through the thousands of glossies and girlie mags while I just hung on his side nervously stealing glances, expecting to be tossed out any minute.

As we exited, some gangly perv in a beat-up overcoat would approach us.

"You men want to see a real collection of girlie pictures?"

"Ge-get away from us . . ." said S.

"No. Don't be afraid. I mean it. I've got pictures and movies of girls, naked girls in my place if you want to see them."

And with a push, the perv would see his prey flee.

Up in the clear light of day we'd breathe freely again, taking in the mobs of neon and food smells and cops and horses and horseshit.

So S needed a little fun after the run-in with the queer.

There it was! A poor man walking down Broadway with a papier-mâché peanut body and top hat, complete with tux tails, and his little cane of peanut brittle tapping the mica-chipped sidewalk.

Taking out his Zippo lighter, my big bad friend snuck up behind the guy and trailed him, all the while scratching the flint to ignite a flame on the rear of the man's shell.

Of course the man inside the peanut outfit yelled at the kid. And his frightened eyes touched me, forcing me to grab S's hand to stop. But shaking me off he pursued his prey, his lighter clicking until the shell had ignited, if but slowly. And then as we ran away, we saw the poor man tear his shell off and throw it in the gutter just as it roared into flame.

So this was no little prank. The kid was a vicious punk, no doubt about it. And I, always self-thought of as a "good" boy, was little more than a co-nastyholic, somehow egging the principal on with my protestations.

Not to explain us away or anything, but, more for the record, I want to explain how he got that way. He wasn't born mean or anything, but *became* that way largely due to his crazy mother.

And she wasn't to blame.

It was those Benzedrine shots she got from that doctor in Jersey who was helping her lose weight. That set her off for four to six hours, leaving the family in a nightmare by the time darkness rolled around.

I remember one winter night in particular. It stands out so clearly because his life as a boy ended.

We had both gone to his house about five o'clock after an afternoon of play.

His mother was nowhere to be seen. Calling for her all around the "sprawling" brick ranch house next to Vanderbilt's old private motorway, we heard a low groan coming from the "living" room.

Once in the usually off-limits room, I quickly took in the white sofa and side chairs hermetically sealed in thick plastic, the curio cabinets and other middle-class trappings I associated with great wealth—and then she charged like a mad cow.

"Look what you did to my wrists," she hollered. "Look how you scarred them, made them bleed." And she tried to scratch his eyes out!

I stood horrified.

They struggled and we ran out. When we came back, after about thirty minutes of walking around in the freezing dark streets, she was, again, nowhere to be found.

So we just tiptoed up to his large room and talked real quietly to each other and to his younger brother, then ten but still referred to as "the baby" by his parents.

About seven o'clock his father, "Sy," came home, exhausted from his day on the truck he owned as a franchisee. The minute he crossed the door, the Benzied-up woman ran up screaming, "Sy, Sy, look what your son did to me," and she then broke down sobbing, all the time muttering that my friend had beat her with a chain!

Naturally, Sy charged after his eldest son. Yelling at him, "You can't do that to your mother, I'll show you." He cornered him in the upstairs bedroom.

As the younger brother and I watched in total shock, father and son came to blows.

Throwing real punches, they fought to a draw, the father satisfied that he'd fulfilled his duties, the son shaking with rage.

And then poor S grabbed for his oversize piggy bank, an object I had envied for years.

Holding it up in the air for what seemed like a very long while, I sensed his life as he knew it ebbing away. His eyes were torn and confused, filled with rage and self-doubt, eyes I would not see again until years later when I would visit him in the psycho ward at Fort Dix after his breakdown.

But then, on that horrid night in Queens, he was just an unlucky kid who threw his glass bank to the floor with a crash, a childhood of coins flying every which way on the cool turquoise carpet.

(As the truth later came out, his drug-maddened mother, it seems, had beat her *own* wrists with the dog chain earlier in the day! Even going so far as to have cried to the postman at noon, telling him what her son had done to her!)

FIFTEEN

Pennies for Beethoven

Morning sleep, afternoon wine . . .
Much idle gossip with women
JEWISH ADMONITION

WOMEN TALKING AROUND THE KITCHEN TABLE. THE SOUND
of a serrated bread knife gently caressing the fallen crumbs
across the thick plastic table cover. Back across the plastic
cloth, the crumbs sifted and sorted, women's voices, didac-
tics towards the ever-changing truths.

I, the male child, listening from the living room, or
from the refrigerator. Listening to the women talking. Not
businesswomen, nor career women, but housewives, later

called "homemakers" (and were they that!), now again, "Mom!"

Addicted to that sound, and today's men too busy cheating each other to bother with such chitchat. No matter how I've tried, I seem to find myself listening to people listening to my voice . . .

It is late afternoon, very late.

I am very well dressed aboard the Larkspur Ferry. A high-speed, yacht-like vessel, mind you, not a dumpy Staten Island plow horse, with a lusty mustachioed Greek concessionaire pouring giant drinks at three in the afternoon. Soft plush seats, but I sit and walk outside gazing at the cormorants and gulls, the windsurfers who've recently discovered this channel, the Redwood rowing team dreaming of the Charles, and, to my satisfaction, the beginning of the early evening traffic crawl on 101 halfway up the low-rolling hills of Marin.

Sighting the haphazardly buried shore pilings with algae growth I think, "God, but I love the water." Always with a sense of loss, for something not quite present. If I love the water and I'm *at* the water, why feel a sense of incompleteness that I ought to be living on the water in order to enjoy the water? Why not "be here and now" and have the water.

So I take my big drink to the upper deck, observe the

bay's green tint today, sigh for the weaker prisoners, reflect again on the remarkable piece of real estate under San Quentin State Prison, and settle down to enjoy the ride.

Clear to Vallejo and beyond, the rich, volcanic wine lands.

A looping gull riding a wind wave not rippling a feather. His sense of energy total and not classroom bought, Russell, my son, eighteen in May, enjoying his last few months of his senior year at Redwood, driving his perfect old Mustang, stealing perfect white bases, enjoying his popularity as the all-American boy.

Tomorrow night's the junior prom. He'll be taking a "rich" girl from San Francisco to her school's dance. She's been calling him for about a week; he's sort of avoiding her, because he told me last week on our drive to the shooting range at the Circle S Ranch, out in Tomales, she's not quite pretty enough.

Yes, she's fun. Yes, she's intelligent. Yes, she's kind to him. But not quite pretty enough.

I tried to suggest that perfect looks come at a high price, that the less-than-beautiful women are often the best friends . . . and then let it go. Our interest soon shifted to the thrill of killer rifles ripping paper targets. The smell of gunpowder, the frightening report of large bore guns, and the crazy types who always appear.

Since early on, I've known I would be no good at business. I lacked the Midas touch, the ability to sell, the desire really to cater to people. Maybe I'm basically the "lazy Mexican" my father thought I represented. He often told me I reminded him of a Mexican with a sombrero falling asleep against a wall. Sunny, I hope, and besides, all the Mexicans I've met have been remarkable, hard workers! They work like ancient Israelites with uncanny stamina, uncomplaining.

Lawyers love to fee me $275 an hour, or $4 a minute while driving through the Sausalito tunnel. Their car phone, cellular Captain Marvels. The higher the fee, the wiser the man, right?

"Pennies for Beethoven" is how Janet put it, when I complained about my lack of hourly consulting fees. SO I stopped as soon as I started. Melted the plastic shingle.

Now I just dream like the biblical prophet my father confused with a cartoon "lazy Mexican."

SIXTEEN

THE SPECULATOR (IN A GARDEN OF NUMBERS)*

HE WAS NOT OF A WEALTHY FAMILY. HIS FATHER, A SMALL shopkeeper, now dead, had managed to rectify his penniless immigrant childhood position but never managed to attain what was known as a "comfortable" status. The son was warned about investments at an early age. On one of their many summer rides in the Catskill Mountains, they

---

* This story is not about a classic financial wipe-out of assets such as occurred in the crash of 1929. It is typical of the losses common to average American speculators between 1969 and the early 1970s. Brought about by an expensive war with no returns, the value of the U.S. currency continued to fall, leading average people into markets for which they were ill-prepared. In this sense, this story is about our times.

both watched a raceway being dozed and carved out of a distant cornfield. The small father lectured the smaller boy, "Sure, they move a little earth around, get you to invest in their scheme, and after they've milked the public for all they can get they declare bankruptcy. They can keep their racetrack."

The small boy believed his father's every word. He worshipped the forceful, handsome man for his ability to say loudly what he felt, not just within the confines of the household, but outside as well. The man knew what he was talking about and told you so.

The raceway was slowly but certainly constructed and eventually operated very successfully. Those who had purchased "shares" in the embryonic raceway corporation were rewarded for their faith with substantial capital gains. The son never mentioned the completed track to his father, though they would pass it each summer over the years. There would be no point in proving his father wrong; he was right about too many other things for this error to have any impact on their relationship.

As the little boy became a man, his father grew neither more rich, nor more poor. His income remained the same throughout the years, rising just slightly with inflation. The small family home was always secure, the children had enough money to attend a municipal college, and the two parents, with simple wants, were able to "go away" every summer to a bungalow in the mountains. The family dry goods shop was managed with honesty and without credit, and provided a moderate but secure income.

The father would justify his moderate position from time to time. As one friend or another would move to a more expensive home, take a cruise, or purchase something truly showy, he would lecture the boy, his daughter, and his wife about his friends' foolishness. He simply did not believe in the American Dream. He smelled a fraud, but was unable to prove his suspicions until many years later.

One of his friends, a corpulent man he had grown up with on the Lower East Side, went bankrupt. The journey back from his expensive home "out on the island" to one room in a poor relation's apartment with his three children took less than one year. It seems that women no longer knitted as they did during and after the second war. The little man's children were pulled out of school to earn their food while the once-prosperous yarn merchant became a clerk in a competitor's shop.

Sadly, the boy's father took pleasure in his friend's plight. "I told you he was overextending himself. All the years he came in here and shot his mouth off. Look where it got him . . . all the time borrowing from Peter to pay Paul . . . I knew all along it was no good."

The bankruptcy of the yarn man served to shore up the position of the dry goods man against investments and credit borrowing. The boy learned to respect his father's position even more firmly through this lesson in reality.

Another of his father's successful friends came to ruin in a different way. His daughter died from an overdose of heroin in an infamous New York hotel frequented by unsuccessful artists.

Once again the man's moderate approach to life seemed to be the right one. Though his children would not distinguish themselves in any great way they would not bring shame to the family, either.

As time would have it, the dry goods man died in middle age of a second heart attack. The boy, named Sam, now a shaky man of thirty-one, had on his own managed to accrue what would have been a small fortune to his father. The capital was not exactly earned illegally, but it could not be said that the money had been earned from legal endeavors, either. It seems that taxes were not paid on income derived from a bookstore that drew substantial profits by selling books purchased from illegitimate sources.

The young man managed to save between eighty and ninety thousand dollars in a little more than three years.

The cash sat in a safe cemented into the basement floor of Sam's mother's house. The young merchant let it sit there without making any investments. He distrusted Wall Street as a result of his father's indoctrination over the years and never learned much about any other financial "opportunities" available to the small investor, either. However, he always heard that real estate was good. A nice, safe way to build a fortune. But each time Sam would make an offer to purchase a small parcel of land, the deal would not be consummated. He would make an unrealistically low offer, which would be rejected. On receiving back his deposit, he would feel as though he had somehow made money, simply because he had not lost any.

The five or six parcels he failed to buy increased two or three times in value over the three years he kept track of their prices. This confirmed Sam's appraisal of his business sense; he was a shrewd buyer but lacked the faith necessary to put his money into an investment. After three years of testing himself, he was ripe for making a dramatic move. He would no longer wait around to die, like his father, while enormous profits could be realized by signing his name to a few slips of paper.

⁓

SAM WAS AN AVID READER. HE NOT ONLY SOLD BOOKS BUT inherited that love for the written word that was woven through the fabric of his people. He had just read a small book about useful plants of the world and was convinced that coffee and cocoa were highly underpriced products of the soil.

Cocoa, he thought, is an agricultural product with good associations. It mixes well into a nice steamy hot drink, is easily whipped into chocolate, and in general seems to be loved in some form by most people. Sam reasoned that the cocoa growers would soon unify their positions demanding much higher prices. Coffee and cocoa were both grown only in the tropics; and the industrialized nations, which happened to be concentrated in the temperate zone, would learn to pay more for their addictions.

Through an acquaintance in the shop, Sam learned of the commodity exchanges, where products of every kind were bought and sold by both those who utilized the products and those who merely speculated or invested on the rise or fall of prices.

By making a few phone calls, he learned the name of a commodity man at the largest brokerage house in the city. After a few cordial conversations with the broker, during which he learned the rudiments of speculating in cocoa, Sam the speculator was anxious to cash in on his hunch.

The broker told him that a minimum amount of five thousand dollars would be required. Anxious as the young man was, he did not rush over with the money. For several days he just phoned the broker to get the opening and closing prices and ask a few new questions. Finally, the broker pushed him a little. He suggested that the market appeared ready to rise and told Sam to get his deposit in an account.

That evening the speculator decided to go to the safe and withdraw five thousand cash.

In the morning he failed to open the bookstore for the first time in three years. Instead, the cash was converted into traveler's checks in six separate banks. Sam thought this would throw the tax people off should they be following his cash flow. He also did not want to alarm the broker. The exchange at each bank went well with the exception of the fourth transaction, where the teller asked Sam why the money had such a peculiar smell. He acted dumb, muttering something about a trip to Spain while remembering that the years in the safe had probably caused his "dough" to mildew. Leaving the bank, he was sure the dumb clerk would report the incident to her superior. He only hoped the supervisor had become used to mildewed bills in this time of inflation, when many people were removing their stashes from little corners of their world.

After the final transaction of traveler's checks into

the cashier's check, a brief subway ride took him to the center of world finance. Following a few directionless meanderings, he found the brokerage house. It occupied an entire city block, was of brown glass and steel, and rose higher than any other building in the district. The young man felt better about his decision when he surveyed the magnitude of the structure. New thoughts came pouring from his brain. "So that's how such buildings come to be." He was thinking: "Men buy and sell, sell and buy, all over the world and this company takes a commission whether the investors make or lose. Either way the brokerage houses profit."

He was amused by the cleverness of the scheme but still felt positive about his decision to "get into it" as he weaved his way through a maze of people in the lobby who were glued to changing stock prices flashing above their heads. At once, he no longer sneered at these people. He understood them, was part of them for the first time. Those phony artist friends of his would not need to know about his new attitude towards them; it would be suffi-cient that at last he was part of reality.

Once on the twenty-seventh floor, he found his way to the commodity broker. They both acted intimate with one another, as though through the telephone conversations they had discovered they were brothers and were now, at last, meeting for the first time since their separation at an orphanage.

For a while they both just sat and watched the gigantic board, where prices for wheat, corn, soybeans, live cattle, hog bellies, coffee, cocoa, silver, platinum, and other items clicked and changed with mechanical excitement.

Sam noticed that the broker was not alone before the big board. He was one of a dozen or so brokers in the large and well-designed room. As the young man casually glanced at the other faces, the cigarette-stained fingers of this very thin broker tapped nervously on his desk. The thin man whispered, "You see that man in the back . . . at the last desk? He earned over one million last year, just in trading cocoa."

The young man was impressed but not astonished. He knew people made that kind of money and here was one of them in the flesh. That the million-dollar earner did not look different from anybody else made him all the more believable. As the young man imagined what the rich man's home and wife looked like, the kind of dinners prepared for them by their cook, and the manner in which they entertained themselves, he asked the broker, almost in a whisper, "He makes that much just from speculating in cocoa?"

The thin, nervous broker educated him. "No. No.

We are not allowed to speculate for our own accounts. He makes that on commissions alone. He is the man who handles the Hershey account. He buys and sells all their cocoa for them."

"So that's how they get their chocolate!" Sam felt much more involved with the real world than ever before. He realized that soon he would be participating in the buying and selling of chocolate, just as this international corporation did from right there in that office, simply by having his broker watch the changing figures.

He gave the check to his broker and watched him walk with it to an accounting office at the far end of the room and place it in a pneumatic tube. Jim, the broker, returned and said, "It's done. Down the tubes, by now. Your account number is zero-one-three-seven."

The young man was made a bit nervous by the broker's choice of words, but he immediately realized the expression "down the tubes" probably originated in such investment houses to describe the passage of messages, checks, etc., through pneumatic tubes, which traversed the building. He further reassured himself by repeating the many names of the partners of the famous company.

Sam made no investment that day at the suggestion of his broker. He was advised to wait "for a dip" in the rising price of cocoa and then "get in." During his visit he was shown around the offices on the twenty-seventh floor, the rudiments of the cocoa market were explained and a packet of materials handed to him, explaining in more detail the nature of the commodity business.

The broker led him to the elevators and told him to phone the next day at 9:30 A.M., one half hour before cocoa began trading, when they would "make a battle plan" for the day's trading.

On the subway ride back uptown to the bookshop, the investor felt elated. He glanced through the booklets, hoping somebody might see what he was reading, but decided to wait until that evening to carefully study each word.

PROPPED UP ON THREE PILLOWS IN THE LARGE FOUR-POSTER bed he had crafted some years before, the speculator devoured the facts of his life. He learned that the New York Cocoa Exchange operated from ten A.M. to three P.M. and that each "contract" consisted of 30,000 net pounds of cocoa beans in shipping bags. For $2,300, he would be able to buy one contract of cocoa on a margin account basis. This sum represented less than 10 percent of the approximate cost of the 30,000 pounds of beans.

He was reassured to learn that trading limits were

established. Each contract could only rise or fall two cents from the previous day's closing price. Each one-cent change represented $300 in the cost of the contract. So, if the price rose the daily limit of two cents per pound, he would be ahead $600 per contract. Conversely, he could lose that amount each day the price fell down the limit.

Sam also learned that there were different delivery months. It being March he would trade in May, July, or September cocoa, or distant May contracts in beans, which would be delivered more than one year from the time of offering. Under the advice of his broker, Sam had focused on "near May" contracts. He learned that speculators like himself would trade only up to a few days before the first of the delivery month and then settle their accounts, usually by selling their contracts, hopefully at a higher price. Only those accounts that actually used the cocoa bean, such as Hershey or Nestlé, would take delivery of the beans to meet their production needs. In essence, these accounts purchased beans ahead of time both to assure a steady supply and also to buy at the lowest price. Speculators such as Sam always "offset" their position by selling before the delivery date. Sam dreaded the thought of making a mistake and getting a notice from a warehouse in Philadelphia notifying him that 214 burlap bags weighing 140 pounds each were awaiting his final payment for delivery.

❧

AT 9:30 A.M. THE NEXT MORNING HE PHONED HIS BROKER.

"Hi, Sam. Look, I gotta be brief," said Jim. "This is the busiest time for me. The London market indicates cocoa is selling from large liquidation accounts and gold is unchanged at $142.50."

That was all Jim said. As Sam soon learned, the broker never made recommendations to buy or sell. All he did was state a few technical facts. Since Sam was at a loss to make any decision, he remained dumbfounded, creating quite a pause. The busy broker quickly jabbed:

"Tell you what, Sam. Let's wait until the market stabilizes. Call me tomorrow, same time."

At the barest audible affirmation sound from the speculator, the broker switched buttons on his phone, leaving Sam dumbly on the line.

That day in the bookshop, Sam went through the financial page of the previous day's *Wall Street Journal* looking for facts in the multiple-columned quotations and otherwise found the paper quite interesting. The business outlook on world and national events was sensible and refreshing to Sam, who had been schooled along by whims of articulate but imbecilic academicians. Otherwise, his day was quite usual except for a more deeply ingrained expression of contempt on his face as he picked through a series of modern poetry for a customer.

Ten years before, Sam had written much poetry himself. He came to sit at the feet of the most famous of the "beats" and once read himself on a rickety pier over the Hudson River. While others thought his poems worthy that night, Sam felt depressed and continued to write mainly maudlin statements concerning the fact that one day he too would be dead, but as a rule he became less quick to call himself a poet when newly introduced to people. Once the bookstore was under way and substantial profits realized, Sam became less and less involved in the world of poems. Nineteenth-century French novelists intrigued him, especially those who either made or lost fortunes or spent their entire lives trying to get rich and famous. He also remained an avid student of biography, prizing the lives of those who achieved greatness through bold moves made at crucial times in their career. Other than these areas, books became mere merchandise to sell.

He stocked the newer poetry more as a sentimental link to his past than for business reasons. Those who were most interested in the stuff never seemed to be able to buy any of the slim paper volumes. They merely read the verse to themselves and left the books more soiled than they found them. Sam never bothered to chastise any of these poor customers. He understood them well. Besides, his business was becoming important in the neighborhood and he wanted to maintain good relations with these people. Already the grumblings about his being a "rip off" were getting back to him and he wanted to avoid a confrontation at all costs.

AFTER A FEW DAYS OF CALLING HIS BROKER, SAM DECIDED to buy one contract at the market price of 64:95 cents per pound. His broker told him the trend appeared upwards, but that if things "turned around," they could liquidate and take only a small loss, more than compensating for it on the next trade.

Through the day Sam phoned Jim four times. He was careful not to say much on his side of the line, not wanting the book buyers to know he had become a speculator. As it turned out, May Cocoa closed at 65:10, just a few points above the point at which Sam bought it. While he knew he had made a good move, he didn't bother figuring out his paper gain in dollars. He figured that one cent up, to a price of 65:95, would give him $300 profit, less $60 in commissions. Below that one-cent figure, he would merely take the ride.

The next day, at exactly 9:30 A.M., he phoned his broker. A strange voice answered. Sam was stunned. "Is Jim there?" he asked.

"No. Who is this? His train must be late. Call him back in a few minutes." Then a disconnect. Sam was curious. "What kind of schmuck is this? Who misses a train when a market opens in thirty minutes?" came the inner logic.

He finally got through at 9:55 P.M. Instead of wasting precious time in anger, he listened to Jim's news that gold was down $3. "All right, let's liquidate at 65:10, the least," said Sam. "That should be enough to cover the commission," he thought.

As the day would have it, Sam was "executed" at 65:10. This gave him a gross profit of $45 but a net loss of $15 once the commissions were consistent, no matter how many contracts were traded. Whether you moved one, two, or multiple contracts, the commission remained at $60 per contract.

Even though he lost, Sam felt good. May Cocoa closed down, the limit by the end of the trading session, at 63:10; and he congratulated himself for having made his decision as early in the day as he had. At least he had "felt correctly" about the day's trading.

As the days went by, Sam watched May Cocoa close lower until it was down to 58:00. The analyst at the brokerage house filed this report.

"Fundamentals remain unchanged. Demand remains

high while production is lower than anticipated. The 58-cent level remains a good entry position. If the price breaks 68 cents it should go to 78 cents."

The next day, May Cocoa turned around, and went up the limit to 60:00. The day after, it closed up 150 points at 61:50. That afternoon Sam decided to buy. He phoned the broker at 3:10 P.M. and told him to place a market order. Jim advised him that a pool of 310 buyers remained at the close of day and that even though Sam wanted to buy two contracts he might not find a seller.

At eleven A.M. the next day, Sam phoned to find out if his orders had been executed. Jim told him yes, he had gotten two contracts for him when it opened up the limit, at 63:50, but at the moment the price was down to 61:75. It seems that buyers now outnumbered sellers.

Sam was nauseous. Each contract was off 1.75 cents, or $515 each, for a total paper decrease of $1,030 plus commission, of course.

Jim did not console him. "Look, stay in touch. This could close down the limit; at 59:50 we may have to make a decision."

Sam was aghast. He said to Jim, "Wait a minute. I thought the trading limits were two cents in any one trading day. How the hell could I buy at 63:50 and see it go to 59:50 in one day?"

Jim explained to him, "It can fluctuate two cents up or down from the *previous* day's close, in any one day."

Sam felt like cursing at Jim. "What kind of schmuck buys up the limit on a day when the price bounces down the limit one hour later?" He was sick to calculate that four cents down on each contract would mean he lost $2,400 in one day!

Jim told him to phone back at three P.M. and hung up.

Sam was in agony. Instead of seeing the price go from 63:50 to say 78:00, and making $9,000 in a few weeks, he might lose that amount in a few days. The thought suddenly occurred to him that for everyone who made a profit there must be at least one person who suffered a loss. The world became grim for him. The old hatred for capitalists rushed back upon him in a red wave.

At three P.M. he learned that things were not quite as bad as he feared. May Cocoa closed down 150 points at 62:00, and his worst fears were mildly tempered.

Jim told him to relax that weekend, it being a Friday afternoon, and to phone him at 9:30 A.M. on Monday morning, when they would make a new "battle plan." Sam asked Jim what was influencing the cocoa market. The broker explained that fundamentally cocoa remained strong, but that it was being traded like precious metals, gold, silver, and platinum, by nervous investors who were reacting to world events. Each time gold went down in price, cocoa seemed to follow. When it went up, cocoa did likewise.

Jim told him, "These are crazy times, we've never seen anything like it."

Sam asked for a key to events that might occur over the weekend and that might influence the opening price on Monday. Jim said, "Well, if they start shooting again in the Middle East people will rush to gold, and cocoa should go up as well."

Being Jewish, Sam quickly retorted, "Well, I'd rather take a loss than see them shooting at each other."

Jim did not believe that.

THROUGH THE REMAINDER OF THE AFTERNOON AND INTO the evening, Sam quipped to his girlfriend, Joanne, how adept he was at losing money. He felt bad about the 1.5-cent drop in the price of cocoa, which in dollars represented a paper loss of $1,030, plus commission. He reminded Joanne several times how good he was at investments: "Who else do you know who could lose $1,500 in a few minutes?" This form of self-effacement was characteristic of Sam during his poetry days. With his successes in the book business and the continual ego bolstering provided by Joanne, who had observed his trait over the years and decided it was not "honesty" that motivated Sam when he chose to bare inner truths to his friends, but a genuine need to be hurt, where hopefully, pity would follow. The sweet warmth of maternal hugging that followed his every childhood upset had made him like this.

Now that he had hurt himself, at least on paper, he resorted to self-derision, hoping for reassurances, which, in fact, followed from his soul mate.

"Oh. Come on, Sam. Don't be too hard on yourself. First of all, you haven't even given this enough time to see if you're gonna make or lose. Second, even if you do lose money, it won't matter to me at all." These magical woman words had their effect on Sam's expressive face, giving to Joanne her encouragement to go on. "Sam, you must learn to detach yourself from your ability to make money. You are separate from whatever you can do." He nodded, she drove further, now slightly conscious of the thoughts he had taught her to believe he was thinking. "Sure," she said, "I love your ability to make it in this rat race of a world, but that's not the only reason I love you."

In such a way, Sam bore his initial mistake. He was still baffled by the drop in the price of cocoa and decided to listen very carefully to the news that weekend, to know exactly what to do Monday morning. If tensions grew in the Middle East, God forbid, he would keep his futures; if a truce were announced, he would liquidate and take a loss.

❧

As a result of heavy wine drinking at a friend's house Sunday evening, the investor overslept on Monday morning. He jumped up at eleven A.M., startled by the time, and phoned his broker. The analyst told him cocoa was moving up and down, changing every few minutes. Sam decided to sell, rather than risk a loss, should the futures contract close down for the day. He told Jim to sell whenever the price was at least half a cent higher than his purchase price. Jim repeated the instructions carefully. "So you want me to sell at a price of 64:00." Sam repeated the order. "Yes. I bought them at 63:50, and I want them sold at 64:00." The order was confirmed and the conversation terminated. After placing the receiver back on the hook, Sam settled back in bed. He felt good. He assumed he would take a profit on the two contracts. As Joanne opened her eyes, Sam smilingly reassured her. "Don't worry. Everything will be all right. I'll probably make at least $300 today, less commission, and we'll get back in whenever the trend upwards looks stronger." Joanne lightly patted Sam's hand and returned to her dreams. Sam felt wise. He estimated he could make several hundred a day just by buying and selling; a few phone calls each day, and he would become a very rich man.

As he tossed the figures over in his mind, an alarming thought occurred to him. He grabbed the phone and dialed a familiar number.

"Jim. Hello. This is Sam. A thought just hit me. I can't get a price of 64:00 today. A two-cent increase over Friday's closing price of 61:75, assuming it goes up the limit, would give me a maximum of 63:75. Only 25 points more than I bought it at."

Jim satisfied him. "Relax. I just found out that the closing price on Friday was in error. It actually closed at 63:25, not 61:75 as I told you. You know how those dumb clerks are. Come Friday afternoon, and they run home for the weekend leaving things hanging." He continued without interruption while Sam fought a sickness in his stomach not apparent since those high school days when he learned that he had failed an important exam. "Besides, you make out OK. Your two contracts were just executed at 64:00, so you profited on the transaction."

Sam asked in an uneven voice, "But where is the price now?"

"Well, it's gone down and up so fast, but right now it's down to 62:50, so you've done OK. Look, phone me when the market's closed and we'll make a new battle plan."

"Well," Sam thought, "a mechanical error. Oh well, I made some money on this anyway. I knew my instincts were good for investing. Look at this. Even with a mistake, luck stayed with me. I sold just right. It's now lower. Who knows where it might fall."

With these comforting thoughts, Sam snuggled against Joanne and settled back for another half hour of sleep. They would have time over a slow breakfast to discuss Sam's new victory.

At the bookstore, later that day, while looking through a new selection of paperback books just received from a trendy West Coast publisher, he was arrested in his meanderings by a new title about Kabbalah. He flipped the pages, enjoyed the layout and line drawings, and examined the rear cover for the promotional blurb. He read, *"Somewhere there is an Adam within each of us in need of restoration, in exile from the Garden . . ."* At that moment, Sam, elated from discovering his newly found powers in the financial world, *felt* like that Adam within himself. He was one, united within himself, in complete control of his universe. No longer wishing for another time, another job, another girl, Sam was all together. Fleeting but strong images of his maternal grandfather who'd died before he was born rose up from within Sam's breast. He had only heard stories about this man, whom he was named for, from his mother. With great respect in her voice, the woman had often described her father's great wealth. Though he had owned several key downtown blocks of Toronto real estate, at his death his new heirs were denied but a few thousand each by a former wife and her children. Sam was in many ways supposed to take up where the wealthy grandfather had left off. If this had not exactly been said to him, it had been implied. He bore the man's name, both in Yiddish and in English, was told that he looked remarkably like him, and often felt, even as a child, that one day he would be like the grandfather from Toronto whom he never once saw. That moment, in the bookshop, reading those words about the lost Adam within, "in need of restoration," Sam felt his grandfather's presence within his body. His own self-image was altered to accommodate the feelings. Sam felt broader in the chest, more powerful, more simian in posture and deeper in voice.

Sam felt other changes. In the short while since he had become totally absorbed by his new reality, he was no longer tortured with questions about his adequacies as a man.

Threatened by a growing healthy son, his father had chosen the most sadistic of attacks to control the boy, all in the name of "fatherly love." The man was, of course, blind to his motivations, yet a keen observer would have noticed the small man's tendencies years before. When his boy was just five or six years old, he often told him about the farmer who lifted a newborn bull over his head every day. "This way," he would explain to the boy, "the farmer was able to lift the animal when it became a bull. By lifting it as it grew a little more each day, the farmer was able to keep up with the bull's growing size and weight."

Like the fabled farmer, he would prod the boy, from

time to time, just to make sure his son stayed on the right track.

All of these thoughts and gripping feelings had mysteriously disappeared when Sam began his speculations in cocoa futures. Now his fears could only be activated by a falling price, his triumphs on a rise. The speculator was no longer preoccupied with his obsessional questions about himself nor anything but his investment. For the first time in his adult life he could honestly say he was happy.

OF COURSE, HIS BLISS WAS NOT TO LAST. SOMEWHERE within, a self-monitoring sensor began to signal alerts. "Can Adam have been created to watch numbers and make phone calls?" Then came this thought: "How real is a garden of numbers? Is this what you have been seeking all your life?"

These questions were soon replaced by others more direct. "Do you really want to use your years watching numbers? Is sitting in front of a big board making buy and sell orders the best you've dreamed for yourself?"

The answers came in a series of images rather than in words.

Sam saw himself a gray-haired man, quite on in years, at the head of an oak dining table, surrounded by his smiling family. Even his smallest dependents were protected by the tapestry-covered walls, and Sam was the wisest elder of the tribe. "How I achieved my wealth would be immaterial to my heirs, even the occasional poet among them, so long as they are remembered in the will. After all," the reasoning continued, "the money won't be earned illegally, will it?"

But then Sam also saw himself as a doctor, doing research in a lonely corner of a lonely room. Like so many Jewish men of his generation, somewhere within there was a latent healer. He had also considered devoting himself to becoming a serious writer who would write popular books about the right foods to eat, how to avoid being swindled, corruption in government, and even a series of instructional science books for children.

While evaluating these possibilities, Sam glanced at the clock in his shop, then picked up the receiver of his phone to call his broker for the day's closing price for cocoa.

"It closed 1:75 for the day, Sam, at 65:00 even." Sam was sickened. Had he waited a little longer that day, he would have profited by $300 more per contract, or $600 more for the day. "Oh, what a nervous fool I was," thought Sam. "Damn, what if it goes up tomorrow again?"

Jim interrupted this self-destructive sequence and asked Sam to phone him the next morning.

All through that afternoon and evening Sam brooded on his quick sale. "That fucking moron of a broker" went the thought at one point. "If he hadn't given me the wrong closing price on Friday, which made me sweat all weekend on a false assumption, I never would have sold this morning. Oh, that bastard." He wondered if there might be a lawsuit in it for him.

On Tuesday, Sam made no moves, or "took no position." May Cocoa closed up by 150 points at 66:50. Sam counted the $900 he would have made that day and watched it fly away from the pockets of his mind. He now feared that the original estimate by the cocoa analyst of the brokerage house would become reality, and he would miss out on a profit of several thousand dollars in a few more days' time. "What a bitch that would be," he thought, "to get into a thing like this on my own, at just the right time, take just the right position, and fail to make a fortune because of a rotten electronic error."

The next day, after going up and down several times, May Cocoa contracts closed unchanged from the previous day, at 66:50.

Sam went back to the original report of the analyst and studied it carefully. "It should go to 68:00 and encounter resistance at this level. If it breaks through 68:00, it will go to 78:00."

On Thursday, May Cocoa closed up 150 points at 68:00 cents.

On Friday, it was down 50 points to 67:50 by two P.M., when Sam discussed the matter with his broker.

"Well, it looks like it might be encountering the resistance level of sixty-eight cents predicted by our analyst," said Jim.

Sam asked him what to do. The broker did not advise the investor; he merely suggested—to avoid litigation, should he be wrong.

"Well, look, Sam, it might correct itself to fifty-eight or sixty and then go up again to sixty-eight, maybe even further."

Sam said, "So I guess I oughta wait for it to turn around again and get in when it goes up."

Jim advised, "You know you can make money when a contract goes down in price, don't you?"

"No," replied Sam, "I didn't."

Jim explained the mechanics of taking a "short" position. It was the most difficult part of the operation, explaining to new investors how they could sell something they did not own.

"Look, Sam, it works like this. Say you think the price of cocoa is going to go down. You sell X contracts of cocoa at a certain price, and then when it goes down you buy the same number of contracts to fulfill your obligation at a lower price. Your profit comes in by subtracting the price you buy from the price you sell it at."

Sam was confused and Jim went further in his explanation.

"Let's say a farmer has a crop of corn due for harvest in a couple of months. There are a certain number of wholesalers who want that corn but must make arrangements well in advance. Since prices go up and down during the months before harvest, they usually buy at what they consider to be the lowest possible prices. Now, assuming they think the price will go up from the price a contract is selling for on a specific day, they will buy at that price. If you have reason to believe the price will go down, at least for a while, you sell those bushels of corn and buy them at a lower price, at some later time. You profit by the difference between the price you sold and bought. It's the same as buying low and selling high in anything, only the sequence is reversed. You sell first and buy later, hoping the commodity is lower in price when you finally buy it."

The mechanics finally fell together in Sam's mind.

Since he believed the price of May Cocoa had arrived at a peak, at least temporarily, he told the broker to sell four contracts for him at 67:50. The broker repeated the order, asked him if he knew it would require an additional $460 in margin payments, and wrote out the ticket for Sam's account. Sam was sure he would make a bundle this time, and wanted to make up what he had missed by selling too soon.

On the way to the bank for the additional funds, Sam counted in his head the profits he would make.

"Let's see, for every cent cocoa goes down, I make $300 per contract. On four contracts, that's $1,200 profit for each cent. If it goes down to 62:00, I'll buy at that price and make 5.5 cents per contract, times $300. That's $1,650 times four, or $6,600. If it goes as low as sixty cents, I'll make $9,000. Then I'll buy four more contracts and wait for it to go up, making $1,200 for every one-cent change."

On Monday, May Cocoa closed down just 20 points. Sam did not feel too good about the small downturn, as he was banking on at least 50 points or a half-cent decline. He comforted himself by counting up how much he had made that day.

"Let's see," he figured to himself, "at $300 per one cent, or per 100 points, that's $3 per point, per contract. So since it went down 20 points, I made $60 per contract or $240 for the day."

On Tuesday, May Cocoa showed a steep decline, falling down the two-cent limit from the previous day's close to 65:30. Sam added up the $2,400 he made that day and allowed his long-suppressed dreams of wealth to fly freely from his brain. "Oh, how fantastic," he thought, "I've finally found myself. I always knew I had it for business. Who wanted to work all these years in a company and hope for some schmuck position with a stupid title. Ah, I've got it now. I'll just keep the bookstore for the hell of it and make a few calls each day and live real well."

While the investor was mentally redecorating his study in his apartment, having the most sophisticated electronics installed, should he deal with several brokers and need a separate line for each, a guilty thought broke through his ego-defense system. "All this money and you spend it on yourself? You don't think of giving something?"

Immediately, Sam placated his god with a fully equipped medical center for the hill tribes of New Guinea. He would also give the clinic a good doctor, a nurse, and an anthropologist, should they want one. Placated by this offering, the god resumed his other business, leaving Sam to his redecorating. Now a perfectly designed sound system, then an expensive antique-tufted leather couch he had seen seven years before (it cost $6,000 at the time!) for the occasional visits by his broker, who actually liked Sam, not just for the size of his account but because he was a really good person, and on and on.

On Wednesday by 1:30 P.M., May Cocoa was down 150 points to 63:80. Sam quickly counted the $1,800 he made and was gunning for a real killing, and was sure the contracts would continue to decline to the sixty-cent level, at which point he would buy eight contracts to fulfill his short position, and then buy ten more to profit on the rise in price.

Everything seemed right. The situation in the Middle East was growing calmer each day. A truce had been signed on one front and negotiations were to begin on another. The nervous speculators were no longer as frightened by an unstable world and were selling their gold. As gold came down in price so did other precious metals and cocoa, which had been treated like a metal by investors who were running from paper money. As the broker put it to Sam that day, as he wrote on the ticket to sell four additional contracts, "Well, Sam, I guess you're wise. Cocoa is acting like cocoa again, and it'll probably continue to fall awhile before it turns around."

Sam speculated that between the ups and downs, he might make eighty to ninety thousand in only a few weeks. His was a true euphoria those ninety minutes between 1:30 and 3:00 P.M., when trading closed for the day. At exactly 3:10 P.M. he phoned Jim for the day's closing prices. "Well, Sam," began the voice, a bit quieter than usual, "your four contracts were executed at 63:80 and closed at 65:50, up 20 points from yesterday."

Sam was nauseous. "What!" he exclaimed. "How could it go up? It's been going down, why the sudden turnaround?"

Jim explained that like the times these were, volatile

markets and predictions were not as simple as in more stable days.

Sam considered buying eight contracts in the morning. "While I'll lose 170 points on four, I'll have made 200 points on four."

He asked Jim what to do. Jim told him to wait for the opening price. Gold was down, things had cooled off in the Middle East, and cocoa was bound to be sold off in the morning, therefore coming down in price as a result.

After a nervous night of sweaty palms, fears of a coronary, which were dismissed as foolish for a young man, and acquiescence to a Valium at four A.M., Sam woke at 9:30 A.M. to phone the broker. He was told that the London cocoa exchange indicated selling from large liquidation accounts and a falling price. Jim told him to get some sleep, not to worry, and to phone him in the afternoon.

Sam, feeling less pressured, got back in bed and resumed the relaxed sleep the drug had brought for him, interfering with nervous impulses to his muscles. In such a counterfeit restfulness, the investor drifted off to a pleasant series of dreams.

Just before awakening at 11:30 A.M., Sam saw a large white bird of prehistoric proportions out flying with two bird companions of the same species. Over an estuary in an African setting, they each dove for long thin fish, which was very scarce. Sam felt an unlimited strength in his breast and wings. As if he could fly by flapping them endlessly. Suddenly one of his bird companion's feet was clamped in the mouth of a hippopotamus. Sam dove to his rescue and pecked the hippo until his friend was free. The three large white bird friends soared over a beach where hundreds of schoolboys, dressed in little blue shorts with shoulder straps, were pouring buckets of those delicious fish into machines shaped like hippos, which consumed the fish by the thousands, their bones spilling from an opening in the side. The bird and his friends swooped down on the boys, who scattered in fright, and consumed the delicious fish while the mechanical hippos clanked on and on, denied their food, until the village elders appeared from afar with shotguns. The three birds easily escaped and gained great altitude looking down on the fading scene.

Sam awoke and waited a moment before calling his broker. By habit he analyzed his dreams each morning. This one, he thought, was particularly easy. "The fish were obviously money—money, which was being wasted by being poured by stupid boys into those machines. I was a bird of prey because my new powers in business give me a feeling of freedom."

Sam had it partly right. He failed to realize that he was

a little boy pouring his hard-earned capital into a shred-ding machine.

Cocoa was trading very slowly and the price remained at 65:50.

When Sam phoned his broker again, at 3:10 P.M., he learned that a flurry of trading had occurred in the last thirty minutes of the session and May Cocoa had closed up a hundred points at 66:50.

Positive that the price would come back down, Sam decided he would wait another day to act.

May Cocoa opened up the limit on Friday at 68:50. Buyers greatly outnumbered sellers, and only sixteen contracts would be traded that day. One thousand contracts per day was the usual number traded. At the close on Friday, the price had stayed at 68:50 and a pool of 643 buy contracts remained unexecuted. Sam decided to place his buy order then for eight contracts. Better he should limit his losses than let them run. Jim explained that although he would submit the order to buy eight contracts at the market price on a "good till canceled" basis, the large pool of buyers were ahead of him and his order might not be executed.

"You mean I might not even be able to get out at this level of loss?" he asked.

Jim treated the new investor brusquely. "You might

have to wait eighteen days to get out if no one wants to sell."

Sam came as near to cursing the broker as possible. "But you never implied this. You never told me I could not get out when I wanted," he yelled.

"Look, kid," said Jim, "I don't make the market. All I can do is submit your order, which I've done, and hope that it's executed."

Switching tones the broker told Sam to forget about cocoa for the weekend and enjoy himself. He advised, "A good baseball game on TV, bowling, even a little sex," and asked Sam to call him on Monday.

Sam did not get "executed" on Monday. As he learned over the weekend by staying glued to the portable radio, the Egyptians violated the truce in the Middle East, and heavy shelling was reported by both sides. Only twelve contracts were traded, while a pool of 1,089 buy orders remained unfulfilled.

By Wednesday afternoon Sam learned he was still trapped. The price was now at 74:50, he was losing $300 for every one-cent rise per contract for a total of $2,400 per one cent, or $4,800 each day the price closed up the limit. Frantic, he smelled a fraud on Jim's part, guessing the broker was in collusion with a floor trader. Then Jim gave him the horrifying news that at least explained the unprecedented rise in price and the refusal to sell on the part of so many speculators. A report from Ghana, which would be mailed to him that day, indicated a smaller crop than expected. Wholesale buyers were grabbing every pound of cocoa they could get in the seventy-cent range, and keeping all contracts they had bought at lower prices.

Sam considered leaving the country with the remainder of his assets. Margin calls began to come in with each morning's mail. Each day cocoa closed up the limit, he was required to add $4,800 to his account or face liquidation. By Friday he had added $14,400 to his account, mainly from cash sources that could not be shown in a bank transaction. The paranoia of bringing $4,800 to a different agency each day and requesting a cashier's check made out to the famous brokerage house required four tranquilizers daily to keep the speculator from breaking down.

After one more torturous weekend, he learned that at last he was out. His eight contracts had been executed at 80:50 each.

He dreaded the arithmetic that followed. The four contracts he had originally sold at 67:50 each were fulfilled at a loss of thirteen cents each, for a dollar loss of $3,900 each or $15,600. The other four contracts, which he sold at 63:80, were bought at 80:50 each, for a loss of 16:70 cents each. At $300 per one cent, per contract, Sam had lost $5,010 each or $20,400. All told, Sam's investment in cocoa futures contracts had cost him $36,000, less the few hundred he had made on the first few trades.

AFTER THE LOSS SAM WAS A CHANGED PERSON. THAT IS, HE reverted to a former self. The fallen ego could only pick up where it found itself and that was where Sam had been about ten years before, when he was a struggling poet. Not unexpectedly, he began to think and feel as he had during that time. He now hated all capitalists and capitalism and believed those in poverty were the only people capable of understanding life for what it is. He felt somehow ennobled for having gone through such hell and, in a way, was somehow more content with his life than he had been before his investments crashed.

But it was not always clear in Sam's mind that he was better off for having lost than gained. In the days following his loss, he would lie in bed each morning running through the figures. The profits he would have made, had he not sold those first three contracts, soon gripped him like a fetish. Had he only held on to them, he would have been ahead over $28,000. Cocoa was at its all-time high. Every few days Sam would phone a different commodity broker at other companies, introduce himself as an investor just in town from Honolulu, and get the closing price for cocoa. It was still closing up each day. Oh, how it hurt him those mornings when the figures would rudely gallop across his mind. His pain traced the following thoughts: "Why didn't I keep those contracts to sixty-eight and then seventy-eight as the analyst predicted? Oh God, I know it was a mechanical error that gave me that low closing price, but why didn't I have the faith to wait and see if the price was really turned around? Every rule in the book told me to 'let my profits run and limit my losses.' I did just the opposite. I limited my profits and let my losses run. Oh God, oh God damn it! All my life I waited for a lucky shot like this. I even picked the area on my own intuition. Then to invest, just at the right time, to see the contracts rise over thirty cents each in a few weeks' time. Oh God, why did I sell them? Why did I fail? Oh, if I had only waited. At last I would have done something right that was really big."

At this point in the self-torture, Sam's conscience spoke to him.

"What would you have done with the profit, bought yourself a 300 SL? Would you have used any of that money responsibly, to help others? You would have been hooked for life. All you would have been able to do is trade commodities. Is that what you wanted for yourself? Would this have fulfilled your dreams?"

After the conscience came the reasoning voice of his father.

"Maybe you would have made a couple hundred thousand over the years and built a new life. But where would you be if you lost everything then? SUICIDE? At least now you have the bookstore and a life for yourself."

Sam continued to speculate on what might have been. Coupled with images of King Midas in a room filled with gleaming gold coins came other images from his childhood.

As a child Sam had often wondered about nature and especially the complexity of the human body. His father initiated this wonder with many stories about the world of nature. In particular Sam remembered his father telling him that men could not create a human in a laboratory. No matter how much they thought they knew, the sperm and the egg would be required. From that time onwards in his life, Sam wondered about the intricacies of the body. Not only about how much could go wrong and did not, but about such simple things as the infinite possibilities of motion in a human hand.

Throughout his high school years and even into his years as a biology student in college, Sam would often drift off at his desk by gazing at his right hand. Slowly moving his fingers through a maze of motion he would marvel that even in an age of electronic miracles, among a species that was sending a projectile 91 million miles into space, accurately coming within a few miles of the planet Mercury, no one had been able to create a machine capable of duplicating all possible movements of their own hand.

Once again Sam inhabited this world of wonder. As a result of his loss he ceased speculating for capital gains and began once again to wonder about those everyday occurrences that, in fact, are the only true capital of everyman.

The man who started it all. My grandfather Sam in front of his own tailor shop at 548 East 13th Street, New York City.

My father,
Neversink River.
The famous
Abraham and
Isaac scene.

I really did wear
dead man's pants!
(Pictured here with
my realist Russian
aunt Bea.)

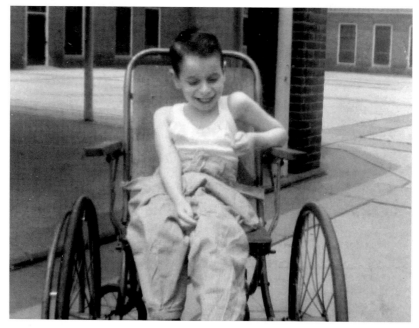

My silent brother, Jerome (in the snake pit they sent him to).

Me at fifteen trying to look tough during my weight-lifting phase.

High school yearbook.

Rifle Squad
G.O. Representative
Chemistry Lab Squad
Honor Roll
Honor Guard

NIMRODS—1957 Queens P.S.A.L. championship team

Jamaica High School, championship rifle team (before kids went crazy on medications).

Plant-collecting years. Viti Levu, Fiji. My son, Russ, with the women who taught me their herbal secrets (1972).

Portrait of the artist as a young father (1972). *J. Weiner*

Viti Levu, Fiji.

"I got my job through The New York Times."
Prints more employment agency and employment ads than all other New York papers combined

Science Consultant

My face appeared in every subway station in New York City (1967).

Psych experiments. Reed College (1966).

³¹p and ¹H MAGNETIC RESONANCE SPECTROSCOPIC IMAGING (MRSI) OF HUMAN BRAIN INFARCTION

MW Weiner, JW Hugg, JH Duijn, RS Lara, GB Matson, AA Maudsley
Department of Veterans Affairs Medical Center & University of California, San Francisco

Kew Gardens, London. One of the hundreds of my ethnobotanical specimens in the permanent collection.
J. Weiner

My years as an Alzheimer's researcher (with my private patron, Eric Estorick).

Arcadia. Honolulu to Vancouver (1971).

Father and
daughter.

Father and
son at the gun
range (1980s).

Mama Savage in her little Queens
kitchen where she cooked for an
army (1970s).

In one of my home studios (2002). *Leon Borensztein*

The Michael Savage family with
President and Mrs. Trump at the White House (2018).
Savage family photo

SEVENTEEN

MY SILENT BROTHER

I REMEMBER THE DAY THEY GAVE JEROME AWAY. MY UNCLE Murray was crying like a baby in front of the South Bronx tenement we lived in. All the neighbors were out watching; think Calcutta, a Satyajit Ray film. The little blond boy with blue eyes was only five. I was seven; my sister was nine. He was packed off like an animal to live and suffer and die in silence, alone in one New York snake pit after another. The "doctor" told my parents he would only live to age seven—he lied. The great man also told my parents "it would be better for the other children" to give him away. This created a lifetime of shame and guilt for me. I became emotionally responsible for discarding this helpless little boy, whom I loved more than anyone else in my entire life!

How I loved my little defenseless brother, born blind and deaf and unable to hold himself up! All those times I would secretly sneak into the kitchen where he sat propped up in his high chair.

"Don't go in there. Don't bother him. He can't see you or hear you anyway." But I would go and whistle to him, and his eyes would light up! I would see a sparkle where the "doctor" said there was only darkness. So I knew he could hear me whistling to him and see my shadow or smell me. He was alive, and they were told to exile him, for my sake!

After he was gone, the little apartment became more silent than when the silent boy was there. For years afterward, I would sneak into the dresser drawer where my mother preserved his little clothing and eyeglasses (they tried to see if they would work). I would hold one of his laundered shirts to my nose, pressing the fabric right into my nostrils to glean a few molecules of his scent. I even wore his eyeglasses, making the room all blurry. My brother! They took him away.

For decades (not just the two years she was told he would live) my poor mother took buses and subways all the way out to Staten Island or up to Poughkeepsie to visit him. Sometimes my sister went with her, but mostly she went alone. The new clothing she brought for him, on each and every visit, was never seen on him. They wheeled him out in the same institutional sackcloth. She would come home wrecked and hopeless for days afterward. The arguments between my parents started to get very bad after this, with both blaming each other, when it was really the doctor's fault. There was some kind of medication given during pregnancy that damaged my brother's central nervous system during development.

Finally, after about twenty years in one hellhole after another, he died, after being attacked and bitten on most of his body by a maniac, housed there with helpless, innocent souls unable to defend themselves.

Jerome is buried in the same cemetery as my mother and father: in hard clay soil, in an old, Long Island potato field. He was the Jesus of our family, who died for my sins.

EIGHTEEN

THE ELECTRIC BLUE
SADDLE-STITCHED PANTS

IN THE SEVENTH GRADE, MY MOTHER BOUGHT ME THE MOST incredible pants. We didn't have a lot of money, but she knew I wanted these pants really bad. It was the "Elvis era." Mama Savage saved and bought me a pair of electric blue saddle-stitched pants. I wore them to school—I thought I was Elvis himself.

On the very first day, a bigger, older kid just happened to be wearing the same pants, and naturally, we got in a scuffle. He pushed me down and my gorgeous Elvis pants were ripped in the knee. I thought it was the end of the world because these were the most expensive, beautiful pants I had ever had in my life. So, the rest of the day, I couldn't sit through the classes. Whatever the teacher said, my mind was somewhere else. My heart was pounding: *How am I going to tell my mother? How am I going to tell my mother?*

So, I came home with the pants, hiding the rip under my coat. I said, "Ma, I ripped my pants." She didn't get mad. She said, "Let me see them. Don't worry about it." I said, "You're not going to tell Dad, are you?" She said, "No, don't worry about it." So, all night long I couldn't sleep.

The next day the women were talking it over, sitting around the little table in that little house in Queens, and they were moving the crumbs around with their bread knives and talking. They decided what to do: They took the pants to a certain tailor, and the word came back: "Don't worry, Michael. The pants can be weaved."

Now, I didn't know what "the pants can be weaved" meant. I don't think they do that anymore because clothing has become something different than it was then. We throw everything away. But I knew from that moment on that everything would be good—and it was. The pants were weaved.

That's what a mother's for, I guess: to fix everything but a broken heart.

NINETEEN

The Fly in the Tuna

When I was a wee lad, that would be between the ages of eight and nine, my father stood up for me. Skinny, polo shirt, dungarees, spring or summer, Saturday, probably working with Dad in the little store down there on New York's Lower East Side.

He would send me for lunch out on the mean streets in order to toughen me up, because he thought I was too soft growing up in the suburbs. He insisted that I go walk alone in those horrible streets and learn how to fend for myself—dodging the garbage, the rats, the thugs, and whatever else was in the street. It was only dangerous up to a point. It's not as dangerous as some kids face today in the average housing project, but it was a bad neighborhood in those days—and certainly different than the "Garden of Queens," in New York, where we were living.

So, he would send me for lunch. There was a dairy restaurant, where they had dairy only and no meat. They would serve tuna fish salads, whatever. It was filthy dirty. If you didn't want the meat from Katz's Delicatessen that was down the street, this place was a "no meat joint." So he sent me for a tuna sandwich. I came back with the tuna sandwich, and my father opened it up and there was a fly in it. He was enraged, so he took me by the hand. He was mad that they would give this kid, his son, a sandwich with a huge fly in the middle of it. He assumed they did it on purpose. They probably did; they were spiteful.

He took me by the hand, put down his work making lamps or whatever he was putting together for the day, dragged me up the street, with his neck bulging, veins bulging, eyes bulging. He went into the dairy restaurant and screamed at the guy, "How dare you give my son a sandwich with a fly in it!" The guy said, "Let me see the sandwich." He opens it and sees the fly in it. He says to my father, "I didn't charge him any extra. What are you yelling about? I didn't charge him for the fly." You know, it's an old joke, but it wasn't funny.

In a way Dad was standing up for me, I guess. I think

that's the one time I could say "quasi" standing up for me, because, other than that—truthfully, I mean—he even took our dog Tippy's side after the dog tore my leg open, now that I think about it. It was like an Abraham-and-Isaac relationship: I think if he had the rock and knife, I wouldn't be here today. Thank God he didn't collect box cutters and that there were no large rocks in the backyard. That's all I can say.

TWENTY

TOUGH HIGH SCHOOL GEOMETRY TEACHER: TWO FINGERS ON HIS RIGHT HAND

I HAD A GEOMETRY TEACHER IN HIGH SCHOOL WITH ONLY two fingers on his right hand. He was a tough guy. He was an Irishman and real tough, but a very good teacher—the kind of teacher who made you come up to the blackboard and perform. If you didn't, he ridiculed you. He didn't curse you out, but he called you a dummy. As you stood there sweating, he might say, "Now what's the matter with you today? Is your brain not functioning?"—that kind of thing. Believe me, you didn't want to wind up in front of that blackboard not knowing your stuff, because you didn't want to be humiliated in front of your peers.

Today, of course, they take any moron off the street, any idiot who has one eye going up, one eye going down, who can hardly speak, and they tell you he's smarter than you are. If you dare be smarter than him, you go to the back of the class. But in those days, it was very clear: If you were smart, you were smart. If you were stupid, you were dumb, and that was the end of it. No one changed anything.

He had a left hand with five fingers and a right hand with two fingers. The two fingers were stubs, but he could still put chalk on the board. When he said to you, "The midterm exams are back," he would read out every name and every score—publicly. Now, why do you think he did it? Because he understood that by doing well, you were proud of yourself and the other kids looked up to you; and, by doing poorly, you were ashamed of yourself and you would try to do better. But now, because the liberal nuts took over the schools, where they try to put perversion ahead of everything else, they have now taken dummies and tried to make them better than the "smarties." Consequently, the schools can't even teach Johnnie how to add or read—and if Johnnie isn't smart enough and he can't focus at all, they put him on Ritalin to dope him up and turn him into a sissy and a dumbbell who can't do anything except sit in a cubicle for the rest of his life and possibly jump off a building when he's twenty-five.

Now, how Mr. W. lost his fingers is another interesting story. We all heard the rumors. It was whispered in the halls of the high school that he lost his fingers—and I'm not glorifying it—planting a bomb for the IRA. Now, I don't know whether it was true, but it was certainly enough to make us understand not to mess around with this teacher, and we didn't. We respected him. Whether it was true or not is irrelevant. That's who we had for teachers in those days: many tough men, most of them vets from World War II.

TWENTY-ONE

HAPPY AND SAD
CUFF LINKS

NO QUESTION, IF I WAS A KID IN SCHOOL TODAY—LET'S SAY, in the sixth grade—they'd put me on every mind-controlling drug imaginable. The mean-faced, clipped-haired women would say, "That little Savage, he has shining eyes and he talks too much. Put him on Ritalin. Put him on Prozac. Put him in a straitjacket. He shows all the classic signs of maleness. We must kill it. Kill it! Crush it!"

I believe most mothers don't even know what their poor boys go through in school. When I was a young boy, my mother bought me a pair of cuff links. They were a set of the thespian masks—you know, one was a sad face and one was a happy face. I loved those cuff links. I'd look at them when I was bored in class. On my right cuff I had the happy face; on the left sleeve I had the sad face. Some days I'd switch them around and put the happy face on the left sleeve and the sad face on the right sleeve.

Many days I was so bored I didn't know what to do. I'd look at these cuff links for hours in the classroom while the teacher was going on and on about George Washington and the Delaware River. I was so bored, I spaced out. I learned that George crossed the Delaware, he saved the country in Trenton, he overthrew the British—I got that the first week of kindergarten! They're still teaching it to me in the fourth grade. In the fifth grade, I learned what a peninsula is. In the sixth grade, it took them a year to teach me what an island is. I couldn't take it!

So, I stared at the cuff links: the happy face, the sad face.

When I got bored with the cuff links, I'd start pulling hair out of the skin on my arms. Today, they would have put me on Ritalin or put me in a nuthouse. They'd call my lack of attention a disease. It wasn't. It was called boredom! I'd inflict pain on myself rather than listen to the teacher bore me one more second.

Rather than improve the curriculum or place bright kids in special classes, teachers today might say, "Oh, your son has something wrong with him, Mrs. Savage. We found out that he looks at cuff links instead of listening to the teacher talk about how evil America is and why white males need to be put in the pillory. He's pulling hair out of his arm, and we suggest you put him on a moderate dose—just a moderate dose—of Ritalin on the first day." That's for starters. Soon, the teacher might say, "Let's put him on Prozac."

Now, I'd be the first to admit that teaching is a tough profession: Keeping the lesson engaging day after day takes everything out of you. As long as I live, I'll never forget the day I first walked into a classroom to teach. Maybe I'll write a book about it one day. You know, something for the students. I could call it *The Savage Guide to Surviving Teaching.*

Anyway, back then I didn't look much older than the students. I had graduated high school at sixteen, which means I in turn graduated college very young. Frankly, I decided to grow a goatee to look older than the junior high school kids in my class. I remember when I raised my foot to walk over the curb the first day, to step into that junior high school, and my foot froze up—I actually stopped midstride. The students were racing past me to get to class and I was standing there as stiff as a statue!

I had no idea I had a fear of teaching, but I did. If you

think teaching is an easy job, try it someday. It is probably one of the toughest jobs on earth if you do it right. So, when I'm critical about the teaching profession and the teachers union, don't get me wrong, I fully recognize it's a tough drill. At the same time, there's no excuse for boring students to death. If an uneducated man like Woodchuck Bill could teach me about life, then surely I should be able to do the same with my college degree—at least that was my view as a beginning teacher.

TWENTY-TWO

WOODCHUCK BILL

As a kid I loved the summer—what kid didn't?—because in those days if you came from a modest-income home, you didn't go to a camp to advance your mathematical knowledge, another to advance your sports knowledge, another to lose your tubby waist. You went and had fun for the whole summer. Without the ball and chain of school holding us back, we were liberated. We'd come alive. Those were such wonderful days: those eight hot weeks when the sun didn't set until nine P.M. At the first change of the seasons, somewhere around mid-August, I remember feeling the impending return of slavery. The first hint of fall was announced by the thunderstorms, and I'd feel the shackles of school coming back. I knew I would soon be returning to my horrible, mean school, in corduroy pants, armed only with a meatloaf sandwich. I'd have to face the teachers and chalk dust and bullies in the bathroom. It was awful.

When September rolled around, I was doomed.

Let's not make any mistake about it: Personally, I hated school. I detested the testing. What do you think?—that because I went all the way through the system and got two masters and a PhD that I somehow loved it? I never did! Learning is supposed to be a discipline, not "fun."

We were kind of poor, so what we did during summer was, to get out of the hot inner city, the family rented a small cottage with all the other families from the neighborhood and relatives up in the cool Catskill Mountains. We stayed in what were known as bungalow colonies because you basically got one room—kitchen, bedroom, bathroom, all in one room—and your whole family was in there. Then the whole "colony" was filled with your friends and their parents, so it became a little village. Naturally, it was paradise because every other parent was your parent and you reverted back to another time in history: We'd play Indians out in the woods and carve trees and make canoes out of birch bark.

In one of these bungalow colonies, there was a guy

who was a caretaker who lived in an old abandoned barn with his wife. That was Woodchuck Bill, to us kids—it was a Tom Sawyer experience. We loved Woodchuck Bill. Bill was unlike any teacher I ever had at school. Man, could he tell stories!

Now remember, he was not a bum. See, today they're a bum; they're homeless. He was what was known as a "hobo" in those days, and there were people who were hobos, who were sort of respectable in their own way. That was his job category: He'd put it on the IRS, like the "what do you do" job category. "Hobo." I don't know what he made—next to nothing. Probably just the barn in exchange for his work.

Woodchuck Bill would regale us kids with his stories. He was a big guy with a big stomach on him. I remember him saying, "All right, kids, come over here." Today he'd probably get arrested just for even telling us a story. "All right, I want all of you to punch me in the stomach." Now, right away that's child abuse today. So, we'd all go up with our skinny little arms—we were nine, eight, seven— and we'd punch him in the stomach, and nothing would happen. So, naturally, we thought he was Superman. He must have been pretty strong, when you think about it.

Anyway, so we all hit him one after the other. We realized we were nothing compared to Woodchuck Bill.

Then we'd sit at his feet and he'd tell us stories. He'd say, "Well, I've seen hurricanes and I've seen tornadoes." We sat spellbound, like out of a book from the nineteenth century. What I liked most about Woodchuck Bill was that he lived in this barn with his lady friend with almost no possessions. They had a few pots and pans, which hung from hooks. We'd say, "What do you eat?" And he'd say, "We eat woodchucks." Who knows if he was telling the truth—I don't know if you can eat a woodchuck.

Hanging around Woodchuck Bill is the perfect example of the education I got outside of school that was just as important to me, if not more so, than what I'd get in a stuffy classroom. As "odd" as Bill was, he had such insight into living and enjoying life and being an independent thinker. He possessed a pioneer spirit that made us think we could tackle the world with our bare hands. Woodchuck Bill is long gone now. I only wish kids today could experience the education I got from a man with his kind of streak of independence! Unfortunately, students are rarely introduced to men and women of courage, honor, inspiration, or other traditional principles. Instead, thanks to the Left-leaning teachers' associations, the schoolhouse has become a hothouse of radical ideology. Instead of stimulating students' minds, they're taught to stimulate other parts of their bodies, from kindergarten to graduation.

TWENTY-THREE

FAT PAT & TIPPY THE DOG

WHEN I WAS A BOY, MY PARENTS MOVED US FROM OUR Bronx apartment to live in a small row house in Queens, New York. At that time, we got a dog named Tippy. Tippy the dog was a ferocious part-Chow who, when I was eleven, ripped my foot open. I'm not talking a scratch here—he treated my foot like a lamb shank! I actually had to be hospitalized and get stitched up! I still loved Tippy the dog, even though the doctor told us to take him to the pound to be gassed.

Tippy was a male, which might explain his crazy temperament. The truth is I happen to prefer owning a male dog. Why? I don't know how to do this in a delicate manner—you know, every once in a while a female dog has a thing happen to her and it's a mess. And, no, I don't believe in having your dog "fixed." I didn't buy a pet just to spend all my time and money at a vet!

Now, aside from taking a bite out of me, the worst thing that Tippy ever did when he was little was to mess the house. Dog owners know that's what happens until they're trained—you get used to that. However, when a dog grows up and knows how to do its business outside, another problem surfaces. Once or twice a year, Tippy would go into heat. I remember how he'd jump on my father's friends' legs. Whoever came into our house, Tippy would try to mate.

This was a real problem because people were always coming to our house. They all knew my mom loved to cook, so day and night they'd drop in on us. True, it was a different day and age: People could just stop by for conversation. It wasn't like today, where you make an appointment a month in advance.

For us, just about every night someone would knock on the door. My mother would serve cake and coffee and they'd sit in the living room and talk for hours.

But when Tippy the dog was in heat, watch out.

One guy in particular drove Tippy insane. I don't know why Tippy focused on Fat Pat, but he did. Fat Pat must be dead thirty years now. This guy was like a character out of *The Sopranos*. You know, he had a size 25 neck. Rumor had it he was a bookie—Fat Pat always seemed to have something shady going on the side, if you know what I mean.

Still, we kids loved him. He was just a lovable, giant sort of guy, always laughing, always good for a joke. Don't ask me why, but Tippy especially loved him, too. When Tippy went into heat, if Fat Pat was sitting in the living room, the dog would jump on Fat Pat's leg and grab it with his huge paws. The two of them would go crazy in the living room! Tippy would start rockin' and rollin' on Pat's leg; Pat would laugh and laugh, rolling his head back on the soft couch.

Picture a fat guy rolling back, laughing as the dog's humping his foot: The women are screaming. I'm busting up. My mother gets a broom and starts hitting the dog. She chases Tippy with that broom like a samurai warrior. She'd yell, "Get out of here! What are you, an animal?" We'd lock Tippy up in the basement. He'd be barking and making noises like he was King Kong down there. Everyone else would go back to the coffee and cake.

There's a lesson here: Unlike humans, my dog went into heat twice a year or whatever. But human males, especially those in college, think they're in heat every night. They've been brainwashed since kindergarten into thinking they're supposed to be in heat 24/7, and then they wonder why they're impotent half the time!

But, going back to Fat Pat. He worked in a seedy hotel as a "night clerk" but he was really a pimp. Now, you immediately think he's a bad guy, right? Listen to this before you jump to conclusions. He and his wife could not have children. One day Pat brought home a little girl from his "hotel." A little girl who was the product of one night's lust with one of the girls from the hotel. He and his wife raised that little girl as though she was their own! But wait, it gets better.

Years later Fat Pat brought home another child, this time an infant boy, from Hotel Lust. His wife's sister raised that child as if he was her own! Years later, after Pat died, that adopted girl took care of her "mother" right up until her last day. Do you think today's soul-deprived world would see a pimp bringing home a love-child to raise until the end of his days? Whether the two children were from anonymous "johns" or were, in fact, Pat's with one of the working girls, remains an unknown fact to this day.

TWENTY-FOUR

Tippy the Dog Would Let People In, Not Out: How Our Immigration Policy Should Be

Now, about Tippy the half-Chow dog: He would always let people in our little house in Queens, but he would never let them out. You could come in, he wouldn't bark at all. He smiled, his half-purple tongue hung out, but if you tried to leave, he'd attack you. He went crazy! You had to constrain him with an iron chain and then put him in the basement. You'd hear brooms and mops falling down the basement steps. He was like a nutcase dog. So, I had a dog that let people in the house but would never let them out.

I think that's what we should do with the immigrants in America. "No Middle Eastern immigrants can leave America without a thorough examination by the FBI." You come in, and we don't say a word. You're not getting out, though. That's all. You want to leave? Go to the FBI—we'll let you out in a few years. You can't go out! What are you leaving for all of a sudden? What, the SSI didn't go down? There's religious tolerance here—What are you leaving for, sir? Ah, you're going back to Pakistan to visit your mother? Tell you what: We're going to investigate you until the year 2020. We want to ask you a few questions . . .

TWENTY-FIVE

Savage's Childhood Diet: Prescription for a Heart Attack

IT WAS FIVE O'CLOCK, LIKE CLOCKWORK, AFTER A HARD DAY in high school, when my mother—God bless her—would put a tray out for me. Oh, was I spoiled. I'm making up for it, though. Now I'm working my butt off. But the tray, the steak, the French fries—I'm talking French fries, *steak* French fries. Here's the diet I had, the healthful diet: Breakfast was ham and eggs with a jelly doughnut. Lunch was something light, like a meatloaf sandwich with French fries. Dinner was something light, either steak or pot roast with some heavy potato dish, topped off with the health-enhancing cherry-vanilla ice cream and a piece of pie—and maybe a glass of milk to go with it. And this went on for years!

If I were to design an experiment to kill a pig in a laboratory, I'd give him that diet, that cardio-toxic diet, for three months. The pig would roll over and drop dead of an occlusion! I don't know how I'm still kicking! So, diet has something to do with, nothing to do with, or little to do with heart attacks. Now, admittedly, it does—because my father, may he rest in peace, died of a heart attack young, and my grandfather did as well. (Well, what about great-grandfather back in the old country? I was hanging on to the hope that he lived to 103. Oh, I recently learned he, too, died young, at thirty. Thank you. Three generations dead young. I'm the oldest living Savage in the history of the family! See, every day is like a miracle. And I also know because I spent three decades studying diet and health.)

That's why I went into nutrition; that's why I searched for the secret to longevity for years in the jungles of the South Seas. I'm one of the original ethnobotanists in the field. What I discovered is this: Not much is known.

What is known, though, is very important, such as which vitamins you take and in what proportions; which foods you eat and in what proportions; and which herbs to take when. What is known is very interesting and can be lifesaving. I'm a fanatic about mega-nutrition. I'm a fanatic about large doses of vitamins C, B-6, niacin, and E, and have been for thirty years. Also, I eat onions and garlic, tomatoes and red grapes every day.

TWENTY-SIX

Dead Man's Pants

Growing up in the Bronx as I did—"the man-child in the Promised Land"—I didn't have many of the luxuries most kids with their hats on backwards take for granted today. My father was an immigrant. He worked his fingers to the bone. We simply didn't have the money to afford more than the basics, so, as you might expect, I cherished and took care of the things I had.

As a kid I'd line up my shoes under my bed at night: neat, like in the military. I made sure they were polished, too. I'm sure some shrink today would say I suffered from ADD or other compulsive behavior disorders and should have been put on a regimen of Ritalin.

I wonder what they'd say about the fact that through most of my youth I wore secondhand pants from dead men. Many of the pants I wore as a preteen came off of stiffs and were cut down to fit me.

Don't get me wrong: My father was a good man. He ran a small antiques store with mostly nineteenth-century stuff. On the side, at least in the beginning, he sold used goods as well. A man's got to do what a man's got to do to make ends meet, right? Occasionally, he would go to an auction after a man died and buy the entire estate: the clocks, the dishes, the mirrors—whatever the man had—the pants, the shirts, the whole deal. You get the picture.

Back at the store, as he sorted the stuff for resale, he'd take a closer look at the suit. Once he got a Hart, Schaffner & Marx suit from a dead man. Now, what's he going to do, toss it in the garbage like they do today? In those days, it wasn't in him to throw out a good worsted fabric. Instead, he brought home the pants to me.

I remember my father called me to the bedroom and showed them to me like the head tailor at Saks department store. He said, "Now, Michael, get a good look at the fabric." I wanted to vomit! I got a migraine because I knew what was coming.

"Take a look at the quality of this fabric." He's working

me like a salesman; he's unrolling the pants on the bed. I can see it to this day! He unrolls them like he's selling me a bolt of handwoven cloth. He says, "You can't get fabric like this just anywhere."

I wanted to say, "Of course not, Dad. They only sell stuff like that for men who died."

You know, it was like special clothing for the undertaker.

Even if I had said something, that wouldn't have changed one thing. He'd go downtown and the pants would come back, "fit" for me, you know—shortened, without the legs taken in properly. They ended up baggy, like an Abbott & Costello pair of pants. Even if they had fit me properly, there was something repugnant about the whole idea.

Like I said, I knew how to make do with whatever was at hand. There's an old saying, "The man with no shoes complains until he meets the man with no feet." Years later, the fact that I didn't have much more than a place to sleep in my first little apartment after college was OK with me—at least I wasn't wearing dead man's pants.

Little did I know that one day those awful pants would serve as a metaphor for the shift in my political orientation. You might find it interesting that I wasn't always an independent conservative. I was raised in a Democrat, blue-collar home. My dad was a Democrat, my mom was a Democrat—most of my relatives *still* vote Democrat.

To an immigrant family whose parents came of age during the Great Depression, President Franklin Delano Roosevelt was "the Great White Savior." Aside from being the only U.S. president reelected to office three times, he gained lasting political mileage with the relief that his New Deal offered. As you might expect then, my father used to tell me, "Michael, all I know is, the Democrats are for the little guy and the Republicans are for big business." In a way, his attempt to sell me on the political leanings of the Democratic party was no different than his sales job with the dead man's pants: He was selling me a failed ideology that should have been buried long ago.

So as a young man, not seeing things as clearly as I do now, I voted as my dad did, since I didn't understand politics. As I grew older that view would change completely. The turning point in my thinking can be traced back to my first job out of college as a social worker in the Upper West Side of New York. All of my so-called "clients" were minorities. Now, I was a good liberal at the time, having had my brain washed at one of the city universities of New York by a whole slew of European immigrants who, instead of kissing the ground when they got here, urinated on the sacred soil and the flag and immediately sought to instill communist philosophy in the minds of the young.

I didn't know that at the time. I was just a wide-eyed liberal kid with an eye on changing the world. There I was, fresh out of Queens College. Having minored in sociology, I figured I'd take a job as a social worker to save the "oppressed minority." I was always an idealist—I still am, as a matter of fact.

But, the abuses of the welfare system that I saw back then nauseated me and started me on my slow road to recovery. Day after day I found person after person who was working, who had a job, but who claimed they didn't so they could get their government handout. Worse, they knew they were ripping off the welfare system and didn't bat an eye. How can I be so sure these hucksters weren't swindling Uncle Sam? I mean, you could argue that they were *oppressed* and didn't know the rules: not me. At a young age I learned a valuable lesson on how to spot people who smiled to your face while robbing you blind the second your back was turned. The next story about Sam the Butcher is a perfect example.

TWENTY-SEVEN

SAM THE BUTCHER

WHEN I WAS A KID GROWING UP IN THE BRONX, MY AUNT Bea was a lot like my mother in that she practically lived in the kitchen. There was something about that generation of women who took pride in the way they fed their family. Sure, most of the time they served a cardio-toxic diet designed to kill off all of the men before they turned fifty, but there was almost always something wonderful in the oven. Day or night, I remember Aunt Bea's home smelled like Thanksgiving morning.

Now, in my day, freezer space was limited to ice cubes, so Aunt Bea would buy her meat fresh from Sam the Butcher. This was during a time when the same guy worked the meat counter his whole life. The butcher always knew your name when you came in. He'd order you a special cut of something, maybe a leg of lamb or whatever. Today it's some kid with open sores and a nose ring working the meat counter, and every time you go in it's a different guy. They know you as well as they know where the hamburger they're selling comes from.

I have to say that Sam came from a long line of butchers, probably dating back to the Mongols. He was this stocky Russian—or maybe Ukrainian—man, with oak stumps for arms, a bloodied white apron stretched tight across his belly, and a missing finger. From time-to-time I'd tag along with Aunt Bea for the entertainment value— you know, just to catch a glimpse of Sam wrestling a 300-pound side of beef in the back. We didn't have cable TV in those days. You had to get your entertainment where you could find it.

So, off we went to the market: Aunt Bea would study the fresh cuts of meat behind the refrigerated glass case as if picking out a new diamond ring. Sam would see us through the little window in the swinging door to the meat-cutting room. He'd wipe the blood from his beefy hands on his apron as he came out to greet us. He'd mumble something about the fresh this and that, holding up a few meat samples like a Turkish rug salesman offering a closer inspection of the goods. Me? I'm counting the fingers to see if he still had all nine! With a nod, Aunt Bea would point to a roast and ask Sam to cut it into stew-sized pieces. He'd take the meat in the back and return a few minutes later with our selection wrapped in white butcher paper.

We'd get home and she'd toss it in the pot with the spices. I remember one day sitting down to eat, and after one bite, she swore it wasn't the "good stuff" Sam had shown her from the display case. This happened a couple of times, until Aunt Bea got wise to what Sam was doing. It dawned on her that he would sell her on the prime rib up front but when he got to the freezer, he'd grab something on the order of dog meat. He probably figured she'd never know the difference!

One day I asked, "Aunt Bea, why don't you just follow him into the back to make sure you're not getting gypped?" She did. The next time we went to the market in the heat of a summer day, she put on an extra-heavy coat, a scarf, and matching earmuffs, just to stay warm in the freezer where Sam cut up the beef. When she told Sam that she wanted to follow him into the freezer, he didn't look too pleased. The toothy smile vanished from his face, but what could he do? He shrugged and grunted, "Just don't touch anything."

I had no plans to lose a finger, so I stood there with my arms folded like a mannequin. I'm looking at the meat hooks, the slicers, and the meat cleavers, fascinated by a world I never knew existed. The whole time Aunt Bea studied Sam like a New York City health inspector. This time she made sure we left with the good stuff—and when we got home and she cooked that meat, what a difference!

TWENTY-EIGHT

CONEY ISLAND WAX
FIGURES

GOING BACK NOW TO THE BAD KID WHOSE MOTHER BEAT herself on the arm: We liked to go all over New York by subway. When we were twelve or thirteen we went everywhere in Manhattan. We would cruise down in the bowels of the basement of the subways on Forty-second Street, where sleazy merchants were selling soft-core porno magazines. You'd see the old geezers there lining up, looking at the magazines. We'd try to look and—"Kid, get out of here, get out of here"—that kind of thing.

We also used to like to go to Coney Island. They had weird exhibits, mannequins of wax figures. Some of them were frightening. One was of George Metesky, the "mad bomber" of the subway. They were so lifelike that, if you were twelve and you had just been on a New York subway car for an hour and stared at one of those exhibits, the guy looked like he was going to come out of the cell and strangle you.

Well, adjacent to that mad bomber display there was another guy: This scared me. To this day I have nightmares about him. It showed a guy who kidnapped and dismembered girls and women. He was really bad, this one. He looked like an ordinary Joe: white guy, ordinary guy. It was a mad time in New York City. Girls were being found dismembered. Finally, they tracked this nut down to a chicken farm in New Jersey. They found a corpse in a trunk under the bed.

This exhibit in Coney Island shows this guy reconstructed in wax in a little room in the back of a chicken farm with a dismembered girl's body in a trunk, and he's got blood on his feet, with a blank stare at you—and they show you the feet and the hands and blood. Today they could never ever display this, but life then was richer as a result. They had freak shows in those days. A genuine freak show is not so bad: the freak had a job. If I went to Ringling Bros. and Barnum & Bailey, I didn't go for the horse or the elephant—I went for the freak show in the back: the one-breasted man; the half-bearded woman (in other words, the people who today have become politicians). In my day they were in the back room of Ringling Bros. and Barnum & Bailey.

Freak shows: half man, half woman; half human, half amoeba. It was wonderful. I liked the whole thing: You eat the popcorn, you walk around, you gape at the freak, you thank God that you're not like them. But, the truth of the matter is, you think, *Well, they're exploiting the freak.* But those who worked in those shows did not feel "exploited." They made a good living; they were around other abnormal people; they had a little world, a social world; they had sex, some of them, with each other. Today, what? They sit at home watching television on welfare? You think that's better for a freak?

So, there's something to be said for going back to the America of the 1950s. Please do me a favor. Don't bring up the Civil Rights Act. America of the 1950s with a Civil Rights Act—can we move on now? It was a better country. OK, everyone's equal, but give me back the freak show and give me back the exhibit of the guy that a kid could see was totally crazy. Why should a kid see that? A kid should see that in order to understand there are dangers in the world. Certain people are really crazy and bad.

TWENTY-NINE

LOUIE AND HIS CRAZED MONKEY

I ONCE READ A STORY ABOUT MONKEYS INVADING THE CAPItal of India. Just weeks before, the deputy major died after falling off a balcony while fighting off a pack of monkeys. The story I read said that the animals were attacking again, with one woman seriously hurt and two dozen other people given first aid in the East Delhi neighborhood.

So the monkeys are out of control—rogue monkeys running into residences. I guess if I go on with the story I'll be accused of simian phobia—and I'd be liable to face a boycott from some monkeys around the globe, and I can't afford that because if the monkeys were to boycott my products there'd be no conservatives left to buy them, I suppose.

Liberalism turns all animals "cute": a bear is "cute," a monkey is "cute." Monkeys are dangerous, with big teeth! This reminds me of the story of "Louie and His Crazed Monkey." We go back now: Ladies and gentlemen, put on your resting caps. We're going back in time. We're going back to the Lower East Side of New York.

Dad owns a small antiques mart. Little ol' Michael is cleaning bronzes in the store basement, and there's Louie the Drunk from the bowery. He wasn't a bum—he worked, but he was an alcoholic. Dad would have him in on the weekends and he'd clean the bronzes—and whatever else he did down there. I loved Louie. Louie was a great guy.

You've got to understand, this guy was an alcoholic of the old school: skinny like a rail, white guy, smoked unfiltered cigarettes—but one of the nicest guys on earth. He wore the rubber apron. He cleaned bronze statues with cyanide! Then, of course, I took over because Dad wanted cheap child labor, and where else was he going to get it? As a result, I got to know Louie over the years. He taught me various things. Once we had Louie over to the house—I'll never forget it—I was so proud that my father took this guy, who I liked, all the way out to Queens and invited him to dinner. I don't know what came over him. Maybe it was Thanksgiving. Louie had dinner with us at the table, and the guy was surprisingly erudite. He knew things.

After dinner we did games, and Louie the Drunk showed me how to bend nails. He showed me mind over matter by taking a nail and showing me that if you put your thumbs on the center and pull back with your other fingers and focus your mind on it and keep up the pressure, the nail will bend! I was shocked because I was a skinny kid with little hands—and I bent the nail! He taught me mind over matter—but it is all molecular, as a result of constant pressure producing heat, which permits you to bend the nail.

I learned that in life it's the same thing: It's all will-power. Now there's another element to the story. So, Louie is this king of a guy, interesting but an alcoholic. Years go by. He lives alone in Williamsburg. In those days Williamsburg was a slum, zero—you know, oilcloth city; leftover apartments from the last century. No one wanted to be there but the poor. So he lives there alone. He's very lonely. He gets a monkey—he wants a monkey! Now, nobody in those days had a monkey. Dogs, yes. Cats, yes. Who had a monkey in those days? Louie gets a monkey. Louie didn't just get a spider monkey, one of the skinny little monkeys. Louie got a woolly monkey. Now, woolly monkeys are really strong: They've got a chest on them and strong hands. Louie is in love with this monkey. For a couple of months they're inseparable. Wherever he goes, there's the monkey; the monkey's on his shoulder, while he's cleaning, and he's happy.

Now Louie was the kind of guy that if he went to a bar on the Lower East Side he'd throw money in the jukebox, and he would whistle and sing and buy everyone drinks until he was broke. I remember the name of that bar to this day: Hammel & Korn. Whatever money he made from my father, he'd get paid it and two minutes later he'd be in the bar. Later, he'd stumble out into the street. Sometimes he'd sleep on the Bowery and didn't care. He lived for the booze—that was it—but he had a heart of gold.

So, Louie gets the woolly monkey. Finally he has someone to fill his empty nights. As I said, they were inseparable. Well, as time went on, we got a call: Louie's in the hospital; he's in critical condition. "What?" The monkey went crazy in his apartment, attacked him, almost ripped him to pieces. He suffered for six months in the hospital. I don't know which hospital, probably Bellevue because that's where they all wound up. The monkey went at him— you don't know what a monkey's like when it goes crazy. You try to stop an enraged monkey without a weapon! He ripped his neck; he ripped his face; he ripped his arms; he ripped his legs; he ripped his crotch; he ripped his behind.

Louie was ripped up pretty badly, but we learned that during the fight, he grabbed his pet and threw it out the window. It just shows you that if he hadn't done it, he'd be dead today. A liberal probably would have tried to talk to the monkey, but Louie knew that the instincts had to kick in: It was him or the monkey. He decided that it was better he live than the monkey. He didn't consult the liberal playbook on how to deal with a crazed monkey—he just fought with it and killed it. I think that's what the bottom line is here, but the point is, even a lonely drunk needs companionship at night. In his case, he found the monkey. It was probably the right thing for him to do.

But it goes back to the story I opened with, which is that the monkeys are rampaging in India. Rogue monkeys are breaking into houses, even into the house of the daughter of the ruling Congress party. They broke into the Indian parliament. Trouble boiled over in late October when the city's deputy mayor fell to his death while driving away monkeys from his home. He waves a stick to scare them away, tumbles over the edge, and boom! He drops dead— falls off the balcony and dies.

So, right now you can see that Louie was a pioneer, in a way, in the sense that he understood that monkeys were dangerous long before they did in India, when they turned it into a sacred animal.

THIRTY

END OF DAY GLASS

I REMEMBER LEARNING THIS WHEN I WAS A KID IN MY
father's antiques store: Let me tell you what end of day
glass is. Don't you sometimes enjoy a multitude of stories
without the distraction of a logical connection? End of day
glass is similar to stream-of-consciousness storytelling.
Some of the most colorful glass is variegated glass. You
know, all sorts of colors were in those vases made with
variegated glass.

"Dad, what's that?"

"Well, Michael, that's end of day glass."

"What is that, Dad?"

"Well, at the end of the day in the glass shop, they have

different colors that were left over from the various things they were making, and they melted it and then put it all together and it became this beautiful, multicolored glass. All the different colors were melted down and made into a thing called 'end of day glass.'"

My dad knew so much—never went to college, but he was worldly wise and knew reality. I was blessed. Not saying that if you go to college you don't know reality; I'm not an elitist nor am I anti-elitist. I'm highly educated. Not everybody who has a higher education is an idiot: Let's not get carried away with these categories. But, my dad was a smart guy who happened to not go to college. He could always surprise me with his knowledge. I was very lucky in that way.

THIRTY-ONE

Working the System

Here's the connection to my awakening as a social worker: I learned that you shouldn't trust someone to deal honorably with you just because they smile when they speak your name. Sam the Butcher taught me that one. So, while I'd work with my welfare "clients," I could spot a phony a mile away. Here's when the scales started to drop from my eyes.

As a young social worker I made something like $5,500 a year. I was fresh out of college and had no furniture in my apartment. I had a mattress on the floor and orange crates for lamp tables, but I wasn't complaining: I had a job and it was a start. After all, as a child I had to manage with what we had, which wasn't much.

I'll never forget the day I visited one of the so-called welfare clients and what happened when I came back to my supervisor in the New York City Department of Social Welfare (or whatever it was called) to file my report. She wanted to know if they had furniture. When I said they didn't, she told me to take out a pen and paper.

She said, "Michael, write this down: They're setting up an apartment, Mr. and Mrs. Whomever. Every civilized family needs a bed—write down $350 for a bed. They need two lamp tables—write down $120 each. In the living room, they need a coffee table—write down $120. They'll need a sofa—write down $300."

This went on for a few minutes. The whole time I'm thinking about my empty apartment and how I could use all of those things. But not wanting to lose my job, I knew better than to speak up as my supervisor told me to have a check cut for $5,327.92, so this welfare leech could have a "decent home."

With that exchange in the back of my mind, I figured that if I had said anything to my supervisor—like why in the world is the government handing out checks to people who refuse to work faster than Santa on Christmas Eve— she'd probably say, "Don't worry, Michael: This is their entitlement." By the time my supervisor was done rattling off a list of "entitlements," the total "owed" to the welfare cheats for furniture was something like what I would have earned in a year. I was supposed to authorize a check to Mr. and Mrs. Whomever to furnish their welfare apartment so they could lead a standardized life. Me? I went home to a mattress on the floor and two orange crates— and I was the professional with a college degree!

That's when I knew the system was broken. That's when I knew the system was sick.

THIRTY-TWO

The Final Straw

THE MOMENT I DECIDED TO GO TO THE TOP OF THE TEACH-
ing profession, that's when I slammed into another ugly
truth about liberalism that put me on another political
course. I left teaching and went to graduate school, where
I laboriously worked on two master's degrees and then a
PhD from the University of California at Berkeley. Major-
league publishers had published six or eight of my books
by the time I graduated.

When it was time to get my teaching job, I was told, in
effect, "White men need not apply." Keep in mind, I had
a nearly perfect A-average in my graduate courses; my
master's dissertation was published in a major scientific
journal (the *Journal of Ethnobotany* from Harvard); my PhD

was published as a book! This combination would have automatically ushered me into the halls of academia in any other past generation. That's when the worm turned; that's when I became radicalized; that's when I saw the true color of liberalism! Here I had two young children and I had killed myself to get that degree, but because of the social engineering of the radical Left, I was told to put aside all of my aspirations.

Affirmative action, a misguided liberal policy supposedly used to promote equal opportunity, almost destroyed my family and me. Here I was a "man-child in the Promised Land," denied my birthright for matters of race. According to the ACLU this immigrant son had "to put his life on hold" so the less qualified (i.e., "others") could move ahead. The rest is history.

I will not bore you with the details or whine. I do very well indeed today, but the government didn't hand it to me. Affirmative action didn't get me to where I am today! It's been a long road of crawling on broken glass. Everything I ever achieved, I achieved with hard work, dedication, sweat, tears, and pain. By the way, none of those qualities are taught today. I guess you could say I'm a fighter; I do not now, nor have I ever, expected someone to hand me an entitlement, especially not the government.

I fight and work for what I want in life—always have.

THIRTY-THREE

WORKING ON
CRUISE LINES

HAVE I TOLD YOU ABOUT THE FORCE 10 STORM? LET ME TELL you. It's a true story.

This was one of the most frightening moments of my life because my family was on the ship with me. When I was a younger guy, when I was on the islands as an anthropologist and ethnobotanist, I took great slides with my Nikon F, in the light-meter days. Those were the days of real photography. I'm not saying you can't do it with digital. You can, because I have a digital camera, and I'm very fond of it. I really don't know how to compare the two. I'm very happy with the digital pictures, but the day of holding the light meter and stepping back—that was another story. Hearing the shutter click on a Nikon F was visceral photography. Those were exciting days of taking pictures! You took slides in those days.

Does anyone do slides anymore? I don't think so. I don't think anyone does a slide, but the quality of the depth of the picture was phenomenal. I have some pictures, for example, of kids—and these were mixed-race kids, incidentally—in the Cook Islands, circa 1970 or 1971, laughing on a roadside as I went by. I started to talk to them, right after a light rainstorm. Blondish hair, green eyes, dark skin.

Because I had great slides, I approached some cruise lines about presenting slide shows of the islands the ships traveled to. I was always in love with big ships. As a kid in Queens, New York, I was landlocked, I grew up in a family that didn't know boating from a lox. I used to drive on the West Side Highway when I first got my car in New York. The great cruise ships of the world would line up on the Hudson River piers, and I would drive by them. They were the most beautiful visions I'd ever seen! Each ship was filled with the promise of a thousand lifetimes to me. I don't know what drew me to the sea in that way, but I said to myself that when I got older, whatever I did, that I'd have to go to sea in some way or another. Now, I didn't go into the navy—fate did not take me there. Perhaps that would have been another life and a great life unto itself, but, as I say, I went to the islands collecting medicinal plants and took these great pictures. Then, as I had children but still wanted to get out there and didn't have the money to do so, I marketed myself in a proper manner. I went to the cruise lines and said, "I can lecture your passengers about the islands," which was true.

So, I got a free first-class cabin for my wife and I, and another one for the kids. I took the kids out of school often, and I'd get the question, "Should you take your kids out of school for a month at a time? They'd fall behind in lessons."

I remember saying, "Look, son, I'm taking you out of school for a month. This is a great privilege to go on a ship. You're going to have to take your lessons with you. We're going to do the lessons on the ship, and you're going to keep a journal."

"Sure, Dad."

Needless to say, three days out and the journal was still blank. The pages were blank; the schoolbooks were still sitting on the shelf. The kids were wheeling around on the deck of the ship, bothering all the old people who hated children. They were the only children on the ship, in some cases, because who else had a child on a ship in those days in the month of, let's say, October or November? Nobody.

So, one of the ships we got on was not a big ocean liner. It was small: 5,000 tons with a very shallow draft that let it into shallow waters, as in the Antarctic. So my family and I went back and forth between Tahiti and Fiji in two cabins. The ship didn't have many passengers. Remember, for the average cruise ship then, a big ship was 35,000 tons. Today, they're 100,000 tons or 125,000. They're monsters! They're hotels with propellers! I don't particularly like monster ships.

So, I'm on a 5,000-ton boat with a very shallow keel. We leave Fiji, and we're supposed to be out there, back and forth, for about twenty days, island-hopping to Tahiti around Christmastime or New Year's. Well, we got into a hurricane. Now, you got a light, shallow-bottom ship in a storm, and this ship is rolling. In the middle of the night I heard a pounding. They put us towards the bow of the ship, in forward cabins—not exactly the best. I hear banging like someone's hitting the steel hull with a sledgehammer, so I wake up and say, "Something is wrong. Why is the ship sounding like this?" I get up, go in the passageways—nobody is awake. Like a ghost ship.

Being a survival type, I knew something was wrong. I throw on a windbreaker, climb up to the bridge, and there is the German captain, who is normally as nattily dressed as you would expect of a sea captain. Now he is unshaven, in an undershirt, and his eyes are in another state.

They weren't in a state of panic, but they were locked: locked onto another place in another time, and he looks at me as though I'm not there—he looks right through me! His hands were locked on the wheel. It wasn't a state of panic, but his eyes were looking somewhere away—maybe, you would say, like a soldier when people refer to the "thousand-yard stare." That's what he had, the "thousand-yard stare.

He had gone a little nuts from the pressure. He said, "Lecturer, all the time Fiji, Tahiti; Tahiti, Fiji. Lecturer, Fiji, Tahiti; Tahiti, Fiji." He had reached the breaking point. We were in a terrible storm, and it was very rough, very bad. I feared the ship would go down. After this experience, I became kind of disinterested in taking my children on long trips on small ships.

Now, I would ask you, if you came from a family that took you away on long trips as a child, did it affect you positively, in the long run, or negatively? Here's the interesting twist to this whole story: It was actually liberal thinking in those days that, if you took your child out of school for a long trip and they were exposed to the world, they would get more out of that long exposure than they would from sitting in a classroom. That was actually a liberal philosophy, which I went along with and ascribed to—and it turned out to be correct!

THIRTY-FOUR

First Boat in Hawaii: Sailing for the First Time

Imagine what it's like for a kid from New York to wind up in Hawaii: I'd never been to a place like that! It was like walking into heaven itself, or so I thought as I picked fallen plumeria blossoms from the sidewalks.

When you land in heaven, you think you can do anything. You are filled with a sense of confidence that only children and the mad have and can understand. But, when a grown-up has hubris, it becomes very dangerous and, in my case, that was true. I had never seen sunsets like in Hawaii. I used to bicycle up to the university, and I would see plumeria blossoms lying on the sidewalk. I would stop the bicycle and pick up the blossoms and look at them and smell them. Sure, I had seen roses on a fence in the Bronx when I was a little kid, and they were soft and beautiful—but this was something unique. The sweet perfume was unlike anything I had ever experienced.

Sunsets and sunrises and birds in the jungles in the back of the rain forest, that you'd never seen or heard before—and you started to get tuned into your own body in a way you'd never been. If you've never lived in the tropics and it's the first time, you start shedding clothing and shoes and leather, and you put it all away. And now you're in flip-flops and shorts. All of a sudden at night the breeze blows gently through your sleeves and you start to come alive in a new way. You go in the warm water and start to feel like the original man. So you buy a sailboat—that's the first big thing you buy.

So, I bought a sloop-rigged boat. *Tarange* was a sloop-rigged sailing vessel, about twenty-two feet long. She was made of white oak primarily and was built in Oregon, then sailed out to Hawaii. I bought her for next to nothing. She was in perfect shape and had no engine. I berthed her in the Ala Wai Yacht Harbor. Most people who own boats mainly use them to drink on and hang out—it's as good a thing to do as any—but I was foolish enough to actually want to sail the boat, even though I knew nothing about sailing. I took it out without an engine.

I knew it was pretty easy to get out because the wind was prevailing out of the yacht harbor. I thought, *Wow, this is great!* There I was on the boat alone. My friends cast me off, released the lines, pushed me backwards, and there I went: down the Ala Wai Channel, out of the harbor, out into the ocean. I was zipping along with the sail all the way out.

And there I was out in the Pacific Ocean, alone. *This is super. I'm really enjoying myself.* Then I realized I didn't know how to get back. I thought, *How do I turn this thing around if the wind is blowing out?* Well, I didn't know how, so I thought, *Well, I better figure this out because if this keeps up for a while, I'll soon be out in the middle of the ocean—and then there will be no way back at all.*

I had no flares, no radio, no engine. All I had was confidence that was bordering on the insane. The first thing I did was resort to common sense. I dropped the sails because that would cut the motion of the boat. I dropped the sails and, using the tiller, turned the boat around— you know: flip-flop, flip-flop—until I got the boat pointing back towards the land. Then, I figured, *If the wind is blowing against me, there must be a way to go into a prevailing wind and still move against it. I've seen other people do it.* And little by little, lo and behold, I was able to—luckily (I don't know whether it was the current or God's hand itself)—get pushed back into the harbor. I learned quickly that sailing is not for the amateur. That's all there is to it.

Those days are over, but she was my first boat. I didn't save the life ring from *Tarange* because I didn't even have a life ring. I don't think I even had a life preserver! That was in the late sixties, an age when people thought with total madness about what they could do and accomplish.

Now I drive a powerboat. It has all sorts of safety equipment on it, but not as much as it should have. But I like powerboats a lot better than sailboats because they're easier to get out. I can get this boat underway in fifteen minutes. It's forty-nine feet long, twin diesels, forty tons, and I can go out on it alone and come back on it alone in almost any wind. That's the good part: just you and the birds and the water, the wind and the land. That's why I go out now, just to look at the water and look at the birds and look at the landforms, mainly—and the seals. I can name every species of bird on the Bay. I've come to understand that every animal has a personality—isn't it strange?

I still eat animals, but they all have a personality when you get to know them—and they all want to live. Dad taught me that everything wants to live. That's how he taught me to respect life. He said, "You'll notice that a cat wants to live, a dog wants to live, a rat wants to live, a mouse wants to live, a bird wants to live." He learned that when he accidentally shot a bird as a kid. Remember, this is odd to a country boy—it sounds very weak, but remember, I'm a New York City boy. To us, it's a different experience than it is to you guys. I respect your ability to hunt for your food—but every animal actually has a personality when you get to know it. They're all different, just as we're all different: Every human is unique, like a snowflake. Well, guess what? So are animals! They're all unique. It's amazing when you come to understand that.

THIRTY-FIVE

THE LEATHER MAN GETS BRAIN CANCER

THIS IS ABOUT A MAN WHO GREW UP AS ONE OF MY FATHER'S best friends in a very poor neighborhood in New York City. They were immigrants together; their parents came over, maybe on the same boat, or they met each other in the slums of New York. They both had a very tough life, and they worked their way up, little by little, as immigrants have to do as they struggle in any society. This man went into a business that took off at a certain point like a rocket; he hit a fad in a certain business and started to make a great deal of money. He moved way beyond our family.

While we lived in an attached brick house in Queens,

he had the money to move his family to a detached house. I remember how important that distinction was in those days: It's like the Buick LeSabre as opposed to the Buick Roadmaster—or, God forbid, you were Rockefeller and bought a Cadillac, if you can imagine. People used to grade their status in those days by their car model and house. I don't suppose it's much different today.

So he moved to this detached house in Roslyn, New York. It was a beautiful house. It had its own lawn all around it (we only had a little strip of grass in the backyard and a tiny one in the front). The carpet was wall-to-wall and pink.

He was a big cigar smoker. We would go and visit; I had a very good time. He would gloat with the cigar and lord it over my father. We'd leave. My father never said anything against him, but you know, I could see in his eyes that he was a little, let's say, that he lost that little battle at that time. You know how humans are—they're competitive! Even if they love their friend, if their friend does better than them, there's a degree of envy in every human being. It's just one of the cardinal sins.

As years went on, the man's business continued to thrive. Then I left home and moved away from NYC. I went and did my thing collecting plants, working for my graduate degrees thousands of miles away—I was living six thousand miles away, then nine thousand, in the Fiji Islands. Lo and behold, on one of my trips back to New York, when I was already a father myself, I heard that this man's leather business had collapsed entirely. The fad that he rode like a wave died. People were no longer buying that particular product, and the man who had a chain of successful wholesale stores lost everything.

He lost everything, and it was so fast that he wound up living where he started: on the Lower East Side of New York in a poor relative's apartment, with his wife and the relative's family—back where he started in a one-room apartment. And that's where I come in.

I came back from one of my trips to the Fiji Islands. I was a young man—I don't remember how old I was; maybe thirty-five to forty. My father was dead, and here sits the leather man. Now, remember, I loved him like another father. I loved all my father's friends. You know how it is when you're a kid in a very close-knit community: You tend to love the people like they're your own. We all grew up so close together, and there was never a bad word between him and my father.

He sat there, shrunken up in the chair in my parents' living room, after he'd lost everything. He looked up at me, still smoking a cigar, and practically pleaded, "Michael, Michael, look what happened to me. Look what happened to me." His eyes were wandering left and right. He didn't understand what happened to him. He said, "I'd rather have cancer than what God did to me."

I soon left New York again. I went back to do what I did, which was to collect plants, and lo and behold, I heard that two years later he died from one of the most rapidly invasive forms of brain cancer.

Be careful what you say: God hears the truth but waits.

THIRTY-SIX

FROM IMMIGRANT'S SON TO RADIO STARDOM

MY FATHER WAS AN IMMIGRANT. HE CAME HERE WHEN HE was seven. He was not born here, but I was born here. He was a citizen when I was born. I'm not an anchor baby—don't get me wrong—but I do have one foot in the Old World and one foot in the New World, so I really speak from a knowledgeable position about it. I understand what it's like to live in a poor household with many people. Trust me, we lived in such a place—I didn't even have my own bedroom in the Bronx. There was one bedroom and a tiny living room with a fake fireplace. I remember hanging stockings on the fake fireplace: I thought Santa would give me a gift.

So, part in the Old World, part in the New World. My grandmother didn't speak a word of English in the house. She spoke the old language from the old country. She was so wonderful! Boy, did I love her. She was so beautiful, very stoic—very, very Russian, this woman. She spoke to me in Russian by the way. I am not a Russian-language speaker, but it's strange: I can understand the language to a certain extent. It's a very hard language for an American to learn. The alphabet is very complicated for an English speaker. I can surely imagine how hard it is for a Spanish speaker to learn English, by the way. English is a tough language, very tough!

But, in my home, my parents spoke only English. To make a long story short, here I am, a "man-child in the Promised Land." When my turn came to assume my position in this country in my chosen profession, they said, "White men need not apply." The positions were closed. So, you can understand where I am coming from. I got so angry that I produced a virgin demo in 1993 and sent it out to about 220 radio stations. I got a return from about five to ten of them. Five of them said, "That's really good stuff. Would you like to work at our station?" I remember, to this day: One of them was in Boston of all places. I don't remember the stations that said, "We like what you did," but, nevertheless, I was living in San Francisco as I am now and one of the offers came from a local station. The guy said to me, "Good stuff. Would you like to come on in and talk to us?"

Here's what the virgin demo said, from 1993:

And now, direct from the towers above Manhattan, it's "The Michael Savage Show." To the right of Rush and to the left of God, and now— Michael Savage.

I'm glad I can be with you seven nights a week because these stories are just not going away. I mean, every day in every way we're getting assaulted. Look at these questions before us today. Look at the questions before us! You know they say that I'm to the right of Rush and to the left of God. Do immigrants carry diseases? Are lawyers really humans?

All right, let's pause. You see how daring this was? You say, "Well, it's commonplace today," but it was not commonplace in the early nineties; it was really daring. It broke open new ground. I changed the media landscape! That's it; that's how I started.

Then I did a show—I'll never forget it. I blew through it because I was under the weather. I'll never forget it: The local station manager called me and said, "Would you like to fill in?"

I said, "Sure, I'll try it." Now, I had never done radio except on book tours. I had done ten national book tours, where you go around and do radio and television. They were very stressful. Along the way I remember various program directors saying to me, "You know, you're really good on the radio. You should consider a career in radio." How could you get a job in radio? It was as real to me as becoming an astronaut. Of course I wanted to do it, but I didn't know how to get into radio.

But let me tell you something: Desperation breeds creativity and creativity breeds a lot of opportunity. I think that fate had a hand in it; this, and God. I really think I was set out to do this from the beginning! All right, so he says, "fill in." The first show I filled in for was on a liberal talk station in San Francisco—it's still there. It's a powerhouse 50,000 watt-er. He gives me a show to fill in for. The guy who hosts the overnight show and is a hater—hates white people, let's say, like Obama's pastor. Exactly, a Reverend Wright! All night long, hate radio: against whites, against America. He himself, of course, is living the high life—as is Reverend Wright in his new $10 million house. You understand how it works. Curse America and laugh all the way to the bank, you know.

So, that's the kind of show I filled in on! I never listened to the creep and I'm never up in the middle of the night. So, I go on the air and I start to talk about illegal immigrants. Soon the hate callers began. I was overwhelmed because, remember what my last incarnation was? I was the good doctor, the nutritionist and the herbalist who gave lectures around the world!

Normally, I would give lectures about health and vitamins and nutrition in America. At one point, I was director of nutrition for a major international nutrition company. They sent me to Malaysia to talk about their products. My audience was all Muslim women, and they were a great audience. These were moderate Muslim women who were interested in nutritional supplements. They received it very well. I spoke and it was translated.

So, I had been all over the world doing lectures and I was usually very well received. Frankly, I was like the "beloved doctor"—that kind of thing. Now I do talk radio and I walk into a propeller of hatred from the Left. I never encountered such hatred from the people, from the regular listeners of this guy's show! That night, when the shift ended (from midnight to five A.M.), I drive home from that station. The whole way home I'm in a paranoid state. I'm looking in the rearview mirror—I thought I was being followed! I get home. I say to my wife when I get home, when she wakes up, "I'm never going to do radio as long as I live. I can't take the hatred of the callers!

The liberals are the most hateful people I've ever encountered in the world. No amount of money would be worth doing this!"

The station called me the next day when I woke up. They said, "Wow, you did a great job, Savage! Would you like to fill in again?"

I said, "No, I will never fill in again as long as I live. I don't ever want to do radio again." Ask them! I'm not making it up!

"Why?"

"I'm not going to go into a show again with these haters."

"Well, how about filling in during the day?"

I said, "I don't know. I don't think I could do radio: It's too hateful. The people who call are full of hate, the Left-wingers."

So they said, "Tell you what: You won't have to do the night shift again. You'll do a day shift."

I did a little fill-in on the day, and I shook up the whole local media. Then eventually they created a local conservative station and I went on that. They made me an offer I couldn't refuse. Remember, I was making a fairly good living as an author and consultant. I didn't want anything to do with radio, but the temptation was too great.

I've got to tell you something else. Radio—you ask

anyone in the media who knows how to do it right, and they'll all tell you the same thing: Nothing in the world of media could compare to the high you get off radio. There's nothing that can compare to the feelings you get! When you do this right, there's no performance in the world that equals radio.

THIRTY-SEVEN

THE DEATH OF PETS: SNOWY STORY

THIS IS NOT ABOUT TEDDY, MY CURRENT DOG, BUT MY LAST dog, Snowy the Border collie. She was sixteen years old. For years I called Snowy "my little angel with fur." I even wrote a poem to her. As she became quite feeble, I couldn't take care of her. People said, "Well, euthanize her," but I said, "No, she's not ready for death." We found some good, kind folks up near the Russian River who took her in, and she had three more beautiful years. She got better living on their little farm. She became the queen of the other dogs—they loved her! Well, as she became very sick, we went up to see her; took a long, silent ride. When we got there she was lying in the grass, and her eyes were glazed over. She was very thin. It was very sad.

What can I say to you? She was a big part of my life. I love the dog, but she didn't die. I whistled to her and talked to her and said, "Come on, let's go for a run." As she lay there, she tried to run, but her feet moved only slightly.

Snowy didn't die on Saturday. She just lay there breathing heavily, and then we took her in the house. I didn't know what to do with her, but she was very peaceful. When I left her in the house, the little place where she lived, I said, "You know, we should all be so lucky as to lie down in the grass in the cool shade, surrounded by people who love us, when it's the end of our lives." It's a part of the cycle of life.

THIRTY-EIGHT

WHEN PASTA WAS SPAGHETTI

I FOUND "WHEN PASTA WAS SPAGHETTI" IN MY ARCHIVES. It was written—let's see—"Michael Savage, August 1985, written in a lightning storm at 40,000 feet over Cheyenne, Wyoming." When I thought the plane was going to crash, I wrote "When Pasta Was Spaghetti." So, you liberals get ready to sneer; and you sane people, get ready to enjoy it because it's a wonderful poem.

The hairy forearms of New York serve you your coffee with a turning gesture, an offering that says, "Drink, eat, enjoy": The wiry Italian in Vincent's Clam Bar, the one behind the greased-over register; the young kid connected, the one who receives his deference from the spaghetti cook, older than his gangster father; the spaghetti cook who looks like an old-fashioned doctor from the Bronx, with clipped mustache. He actually pulls some noodles out of the pot and eats them as they cook, looking to the grimy ceiling for his tender answer. Well, they used to call it "spaghetti." Now it's "pasta" at ten dollars a plate. The smoky windows of Romeo's Spaghetti now offer radios and knickknacks. It was fifty cents a plate then. In neon letters that you couldn't miss, even through a fogged-over window on a cold winter's eve, there was life: marinara sauce that stuck to the seat; noodles as long as your young arm; meatballs as fluffy as your dreams of them; bread on the table that you'd eat against your parents' admonition that "the meal was a-coming, the meal was a-coming." And men, some burly with black hairy forearms, whose smiles scared you. And little skinny guys with the look of murder on their faces, and people who slurped their spaghetti straight to their mouths from the plate, in one motion like Chinese shoveling rice in the mouth with clicking sticks. That was gusto before it became a beer ad. That was taste before it became a synonym for fashion. That was spaghetti before it became pasta.

THIRTY-NINE

Separate Bedrooms

I READ A STORY ONCE ABOUT THE NUMBER OF MARRIED couples in the United States that choose to sleep in separate bedrooms. A survey showed that this trend is increasingly popular because of marital tension and disturbances in sleep as a result of sharing a bedroom. They're not calling it a separate bedroom, because the people are embarrassed to admit it. They call it a "flex suite" instead, to avoid any embarrassment.

Let me tell you a little secret about that: It's only poor couples who sleep in the same bed for their whole lives, generally. Not everybody, don't get me wrong. But generally it's a mark of poverty to have to share a bed with someone your whole life.

The fact of the matter is, if you study the history of this—let's start with royalty. They never shared the same bedroom, never mind the same bed! We're not talking about in the beginning phases, when they were in the ninety days of marital heat—that's an understood fact. The ninety-day period is over after ninety, ninety-one days according to every study that's ever been done. Ninety days of insanity, then by ninety-one days, it's already over. It goes on to a certain extent, but after ninety days you have to live with this person.

So, first it starts out as twin beds in the same room, very close to each other, with a little nightstand. Then it's not so much twin beds—you get the bigger beds in the same room. Then if you have a little money . . . That's how it works; that's the fact of the matter. There's no shame in it! You can still get together when you want, but you have two different lives, two different minds. Why do you have to share every second in the bedroom? What, that's some sacred place to be together? The way people are today, individually, they don't want to be in the same room—and, by the way, this is not limited to America. I'll give you an example, an anthropological experience about men and women.

In Fiji—let's go back to the years I was living in Fiji, in the village. This is a delicate subject. The men had a men's house and the women had a women's house. When a woman went through her monthly cycles, she went into the women's house with the other women. The men didn't want to be around them during that time! Now, what does that make the men in Fiji? Does it make them sexist? Does it make them whatever "ist" you want to call it? They knew, from their culture, that they didn't want to be around the women at that time, for whatever the reasons were. And I got news for you: The women would rather be with their friends at that time, too! So, the guys went over with their friends in their separate house, they all hung out, slept in the same big straw hut—and the women slept together! That's how they did it in Fiji. I'm giving you one example.

So, this whole idea of how to raise a child—or how to live with a woman or, for a woman, how to live with a man—there's no set rules in this area. A lot of what we see going on today is devolution, not evolution. The people don't even actually understand how to live with each other or how to raise children. And what they always do is try an extremely tolerant methodology: People think that by going with liberal social mores it's going to work, and it often doesn't.

What you have to do is go back to the traditional methods of raising children and the traditional methods of living in the same household—man and woman, woman and man.

FORTY

Political Museums and the Downfall of Western Culture

Question is this: Do you still go to museums or have museums become "museums" in the U.S.A.? I used to live in museums. Because I grew up in my dad's antiques store looking at art, I spent a lot of time in museums—I always have. I stopped going years ago, though, when the AIDS racketeers started dominating San Francisco's collections and turned everything in museums into a sort of "plea" for a special subpopulation of the American people. I couldn't take it anymore, so I stopped going.

Too many exhibits have become propaganda, not art.

They put a basket from Guatemala next to a Rembrandt and they tell you they're culturally equal! Nevertheless, the European collections are still there—and they still stand out, and they are still worth going to see.

So, let me begin at the end: I recently went to the de Young and came out feeling enlightened. I use the word "enlightened" in the way it truly was written and meant to be understood: I felt lighter inside. My spirit was lifted from association with great art. I stood nose to nose with Hopper and Church and other great artists—you know, our sight an inch from the oil paint is an astonishing thing to behold. You can literally feel the movements of the brush. It does something to your mind that you can't compare with anything else—certainly not television or a movie.

So, I saw some of my favorite old paintings. They were amazingly fabulous. I just love the intelligent, young families with young children; sadly, they're mainly Europeans. There are very few American families; it's mainly French families that still take their young children to the museums, as I did my children.

Yenta is a term in American slang denoting a "busybody." There was an exhibit in the museum that was just breathtakingly, frighteningly hard to believe it was in a museum, about this San Francisco–native yenta with good taste in fashion. When I saw this I thought, *Now this can't be. They can't be doing this.* But, yes, they were doing it. Here's a woman I never heard of and her dresses were in showcases in the museum! But wait, it gets worse: There was a whole glass case devoted to this woman's shoes. Her shoes! So, I stood there laughing out loud. People thought I was crazy! I said, "My God, it's every yenta's dream. There they are, the yenta's shoes, under glass in a museum after she's dead."

So, a guard came over to me and whispered, "You're one-hundred-percent right. Don't tell anyone I said so." He couldn't believe it, either! I said, "In all the years you've been in a museum, have you ever seen a woman's shoes put on display in a showcase?" He said, "Never." So I said, "This exhibit is the ultimate 'nothing.'" It's the ultimate nothing. You have to ask yourself, "Who is in charge of our museums, that they would put a woman's dresses in the showcase—and her shoes?"

This woman was living on her father's money and her husband's money—probably did nothing in her life except wear clothing. I'm editorializing, mind you: This is my opinion. This clothing exhibit was in a major museum in the U.S.A. This is what it's come down to, with the assault upon our institutions in this country by the illegitimate Left. This is the kind of garbage they're showing! They put this exhibit in an American museum, next to paintings by Hopper, paintings by Church, paintings by the most genius artists of our historical past. They put a yenta's clothing in a showcase.

I could not believe that this is what has become considered worthy of showing in our museums. How did this happen to American culture? Now remember, I grew up in museums. I spent many, many, many a happy rainy day playing hooky at the Metropolitan Museum in New York— thousands of hours in the Metropolitan, wandering, before it became a zoo. Wandering alone on rainy Tuesdays, or Wednesdays, or Thursdays, in soiled raincoats; wandering the endless halls before it filled up with the Euro-hordes and forced schoolchildren; wandering through these halls of the museum.

It does not make me an art expert by any means, but then, there are no art experts. When it comes to taste, the fact of the matter is, there are people who are expert in certain areas of art and they could probably tell you something about a painting that you don't already know, but, ultimately, you're the best judge of whether a piece of art is really a piece of art. You are the only judge of whether a piece of art is a piece of art! It's the average man who is the judge. It's not the effete academic who will determine whether a piece of art is a piece of art any more than an academic can tell you whether a baseball player is really a great baseball player. It's the fan in the stadium that will tell you whether he's a great baseball player.

I need a day in the museum, I thought before going. The positive side of this outing was seeing the great paintings by Hopper, the great paintings by Church, the great paintings by so many other artists that I grew up salivating over. After seeing these, I must tell you, I wandered into the Oceania collection, which is the Pacific Islands collection. I spent many years during my time in the South Pacific collecting mud masks and shields, and I am talking about collecting them in the late sixties and early seventies, when they were really exquisite. They were museum pieces. I have them somewhere—I don't even know where I put them—in storage.

When you walk around the Oceania collection—I'm talking about the Pacific Islands: Polynesia, Melanesia, Micronesia, the islands of the deep South Pacific and the western Pacific. Observing these death masks in the showcases—where there are human skulls in a showcase called "ancestral masks," where they take the head, the skull of an ancestor, put feathers and mud around it, and put it in their house as a totem—a number of thoughts and feelings come to mind. (A) They're spooky and eerie, and the person is in there and I can feel the person's spirit

in the showcase, and (b) they don't belong in the showcase. They should be returned to New Guinea where they
came from.

If the Greeks or Romans or Italians can demand their
art back from the crooks at the Getty Museum then certainly the poor people of New Guinea can demand to get
back the masks that contain actual skulls from people who
lived. But let me get to the next point—

You stand there and look at some of these Oceanic art-
works. First, you can dismiss them as primitive and not
really great if you don't really understand what they are,
but if you do understand what they are, you actually see
the greatness in some of these pieces of mud and feathers
and bone and shell. Now, that's an area that I really could
talk about for hours.

The power of "primitive" art is great—and I'm not
talking about the garbage that they carve in the Philip-
pines now for the tourists or the junk that they're selling in
the streets of Tahiti. That's all junk. I'm talking about the
stuff that was collected, let's say, up to 1920, or even 1940.
Pre–World War II Oceanic art is astonishing in terms of its
power.

FORTY-ONE

THE TIME SHELTER

I WAS RECENTLY ON THE STREETS OF NORTH BEACH, THE once-Italian district of San Francisco. Now it's the home to bums and Chinese, with a remnant of Little Italy left— the Little Italy amusement park, North Beach. But forty years ago when I came to San Francisco, there used to be women dressed in black—old, lean Italian women. They used to gossip with each other on the street, whispering. I loved it. Being the kind of guy I am, I would once in a while go up and talk to them. (Wherever I've been in the world, I've had the capacity to go up to strangers. I always get into good conversations for some reason.) I don't know how the conversation arose. I was talking to one of the old women—she must have been a good ninety-five, probably Sicilian. I said to her, "Mama, what do you do for health?"

She says to me, "There's hardly anything wrong with a person that a little coffee, a little wine, and a little garlic can't cure."

I agree with her 100 percent. Of course, I must add a few things to that mixture: Like, it's not a *little* wine; it's more than a little wine. It's not a *little* garlic; it's a lot more than a little garlic. And there are other things that I like to do, but for her, it worked. They were beautiful old women. They're gone—you don't see them anymore.

FORTY-TWO

BEING DECENT IS
NOT LOVE

IF YOU ARE DECENT TO OTHERS, THEN YOU'RE DECENT TO yourself. You feel better. I don't want to say if you love others, you love yourself, because I think the word *love* is overused—and it's not the right verb anyway. In Latin there are sixteen verbs for love. We have one verb for love and we get mixed up: I love my girlfriend, I love my mother, I love my pizza, I love my bike, I love my car, and I love my dog. In the Latin there are sixteen different verbs for these emotions.

Here, we're so limited by the choice of the one verb *love* that we mix up a pizza with our mother and our girlfriend and our bicycle! That's why I avoid the word *love* altogether—I don't like it. It makes me uncomfortable. You love me? You love me, honey? Everything in America is "love."

I'm an Old World kind of guy. I was raised with it. My father never believed in the word *love*. He got mad if you said "love" around him. He knew it was b.s. "I love everybody." You can't love strangers that you don't know, but you can be nice to them. You don't have to go out of your way to be a fool.

My line is: If you are decent to other people, you're decent to yourself. You feel better. Try it for a day. Look, let's say you're a typical, mean S.O.B. You cut people off, you give them the finger, you're an obnoxious, cheap, hateful human being—the average man in other words. Try one day to be decent to strangers. See the power of human kindness.

FORTY-THREE

MAN IS A CREATURE OF REASON

I WAS READING THE TEACHINGS OF BUDDHA, CALLED *The Way of Practical Attainment*. Here's one; tell me whether this applies to you. It doesn't matter what your religion is.

> A man who chases after fame and wealth and love af-
> fairs is like a child who licks honey from the blade of
> a knife: while he is tasting the sweetness of honey he
> has to risk hurting his tongue. He is like a man who
> carries a torch against the strong wind: the flame will
> surely burn his hands and face. People love their ego-
> istic comfort, which is a love of fame and praise, but

fame and praise are like incense that consumes itself
and soon disappears. If people chase after honors and
public acclaim and leave the way of truth, they're in
serious danger and will soon have cause for regret.

It's beautiful poetry, I've got to tell you that. It's universal in the sense that it crosses over to whatever your religion might be. Even if you're an atheist, you can find these rules somewhat reasonable to live by, unless you don't believe in any rules at all because you're so wild and free. Oh, we understand that—we understand that people who aren't religious are just "wild and free" and they're so progressive in their freedom and their liberation. As George Orwell said, "The more people chant about their freedom and how free they are, the more loudly I hear their chains rattling."

"A scripture that is not read with sincerity soon becomes covered with dust." Who does that sound like? You remember the staged Bibles of the Clintons? Remember that overly large Bible they used to carry on Sundays, that was made for them in Hollywood, on a Hollywood set? It was one-and-a-half to two-and-one-half times the size of an ordinary Bible. The cross was so big you couldn't miss it from a hundred yards away! "A scripture that is not read with sincerity soon becomes covered with dust." "A house that is not fixed when it needs repairing becomes filthy; so an idle man soon becomes defiled."

Why do you think each nation, each people, and each religion has these writings? What is the purpose of any of this? If you were just left to your wants and to your needs and what you're moaning about—"Oh, I don't have this, I don't have that. I don't have an airplane. Oh, I don't have a girlfriend. Oh, I don't have ten girlfriends. Oh, I don't have a house in Aspen next to Dianne Feinstein, the war profiteer. Oh, I'm not him. Oh, I'm not invited there"—you're going to just moan and groan through your whole life!

You have to understand that there are millions, tens of millions, of people like you on the earth, going through exactly the same moanings and groanings and that you have to find your way out of it without taking a pill, or using drugs. There's nothing wrong with taking a pill if you need it, or taking a bicycle ride—trust me on that one—but that's not the point. That shouldn't be your only way out of a problem. If man is anything, he is a creature of reason. Do you understand what I'm saying to you? How do you define man? Man is an animal who reasons.

Let's say you don't believe in God, our Creator, so you're into mechanism. You say, "Well, we're only animals." We have animal bodies, but you have to admit that we are animals who reason. So, therefore, if a man reasons—or a man *can* reason—then he can think his way out of almost any problem that he puts himself in. All these problems, by the way, are temporal—small problems, these wants and these needs. If you thought yourself into them, you should be able to think your way out of most of them.

But, you can't do it all on your own. Some of them you could try on your own, but you're probably not going to be able to succeed. See, that's when people start to turn to the scriptures or to the teachings of Buddha or to another religion—Zen Buddhism, or yoga.

To me it all looks like a burlesque when I look into a yoga studio: I feel like I'm from another planet. If you're doing yoga, why do you have to wear a costume that shows your private parts to everyone in the room? Can't you do yoga wearing something that's a little more dignified, I ask myself? I mean, if it's purely for the spirit, to get control of the spirit, why are they wearing a show-all pair of tights and they're on their hands and knees?

See, you have to find the answer somewhere else than in your own head. In other words, we are creatures, we are animals that reason, so we can use reason to get out of any hole that we find ourselves in. But, we don't have to write the scriptures to get us out of that hole. Let's go to the people who thought this through ten thousand years ago, five thousand years ago, a thousand years ago. We don't need some "author" who was on TV to get us out of it! He probably stole it from one of these books anyway and repackaged it! You may as well go back to the original guys who wrote the stuff.

This is another from the teaching of Buddha, and the reason I'm quoting it is not because I'm a Buddhist but because it makes sense. And so, here's another one of the practical guides: "The duty of a ruler is to protect his people." How's that for a starter, Mr. Obama? "The duty of a ruler is to protect his people," and many of us would say he is. OK. "He is the parent of his people and he protects them by his laws." Well, when Obama uses drones to kill, we start to wonder what kind of parent he might be.

The Buddhist teaching goes on:

> He must raise his people like parents raise their chil-
> dren, giving a dry cloth to replace a wet one without
> waiting for the child to cry. In like manner, the ruler
> must remove suffering and bestow happiness with-
> out waiting for people to complain. Indeed, his ruling
> is not perfect until his people abide in peace. They
> are his country's treasure.

I love that one: The people are a nation's treasure. You hear what I'm saying to you? We are the treasure of America! You and I are the treasure of America: not the senators, not the congressmen, not the media. We are the treasure of America!

"Therefore a wise ruler is always thinking of his people and does not forget them even for a moment." Wouldn't you like to believe that? Wouldn't you like to wake up or go to sleep knowing that your wise rulers are always thinking of you and don't forget you for a moment other than to deceive you and to fleece you?

> *He thinks of their hardships and plans for their prosperity. To rule wisely, he must be advised about everything: about water, about drought, about storms, about rain. He must know about crops, the chances for a good harvest, people's comforts and their sorrows. To be in a position to rightly award, punish, or praise, he must be thoroughly informed as to the guilt of bad men and the merits of good men.*

I think you've got the picture. That's why I've included various religious writings. When you hear people say they're the wrong gender trapped in a body, for example—the current psychosis among the transgender crowd—he's a woman trapped in a man's body so he's going to go to a surgeon to cut off his penis. To me, that's total insanity! The doctor should be arrested for malpractice, and the person who thinks that about himself should be given antipsychotic medication or put into a mental ward.

Never before in history has a man awakened and said, "I'm a woman in a man's body." Never! This is propaganda. There may have been homosexuals on earth from the beginning of time and there may be homosexuals on earth till the end of time—we understand that—but to say you're a woman in a man's body—can't you just be a man who likes men? Why must you say you're a woman in a man's body? Where'd that come from? That comes from the psychosis of the psychiatric movement that has convinced thousands of marginally sane people that they're men born in women's bodies!

But just as I can read Buddhist scripture and I don't have to be a Buddhist, I don't have to say I'm a Buddhist trapped in an American's body. I don't have to become a Buddhist to read the Buddhist tracts. You don't have to shift religions just to read the other religion's books. You don't have to say, "Now I'm trapped in the wrong religion." You were born in a religion. That's the religion that's right for you. It's genetic! It's part of your genetic code. Your parents were that religion. Going back many generations. It's in your genetic code. It's encoded within your mind and your psyche—and you're never going to find peace in another religion! You're always going to be confused. You may find temporary peace by saying, "Oh, I'm a Buddhist." Stop trying to change religions, jumping from one to another like you'd jump between hobbies.

Have you ever seen these liberal American "Buddhists" walking around? They don't even know what Buddhism means! They use it as a form of ego pride. They're trying to show they're different than you, better than you—that they've evolved from, let's say, Catholicism into Buddhism.

Now, the first teaching of Buddhism will tell you that you can't use a religion as a matter of pride, as the Iranian Hitler did. He used his religion as a matter of pride. He was misusing his own religion by bashing us over the head with it and saying, "The world will not be peaceful until you all accept my religion." To me, that's the mark of a person who doesn't even understand his own religion. You can't misuse your religious book and say, "You must be like *me*, you must follow *my* religion, or there will be no peace on earth!" You're abusing your religious teachings! It's the opposite of your religion to do that!

But nobody said that to Iran's Hitler. Obama had the chance to do that in the United Nations. He's our leader; he could have gotten up there and said ten things we would have remembered. He could have had somebody write a speech for him that said, "We have a visitor to America today who is using his religion in a prideful manner, trying to tell us that unless we convert to his religion, there will be no peace on earth. This is the act of a lowly man who is hostile to the rest of the world, and it has no place in the United Nations, where humanism and humanitarianism should prevail—not threats." He could have said that. The world would have stood up and cheered, and said, "What got into him? Who wrote that speech for him?"

And that's part of the problem. It goes back to this core statement: that national pride has never been this low in my lifetime. I've never seen national pride at this low point. We are at the lowest point of national pride that I can ever remember. Tell me if I'm wrong: Can you remember a day that national pride was lower than it is today? On September 12, 2001, it was higher than it is today! The day after the Islamic murderers hit us, the nation was very proud because we knew we were going to fight back and we were going to beat them—but we haven't beaten them for all the cowardly reasons that we know to be in play.

But, we were proud to be Americans that day. We all came together. We were prouder the day *after* we were hit than we are today.

FORTY-FOUR

TALKING TO A BUM
ABOUT GOD

I DON'T KNOW HOW MANY HOUSES OF WORSHIP I'VE TRIED IN
my life that I've walked out of. I walked out of them sometimes because I was bored, sometimes because I thought
their politics were too far to the Left. I've walked out of
many houses of worship. In fact, I never found one that I
liked. And yet, I'm a man who believes in God. Why? Who
am I *not* to believe in God? Who am I to say, "I don't believe in God"? What do you think I am: bigger than God?
"Do you think I created myself?" a man once said to me.
"Follow your logic in your own head," a homeless man
said to me.

I was once into, more so than now, talking to strangers. I was the wandering man who would talk to weird people, figuring they held the truth, or some truth. Now I hold my own truths. I don't need to talk to strangers to form my opinions. I can come up with my own, but when I was younger, I talked to a lot of odd people. One of them was an itinerant man. You'd call him a bum, but he wasn't really because he wasn't really dirty. He wasn't disheveled; he didn't look like a homeless man, but he was. He had a backpack and long white hair. He wasn't particularly clean and he wasn't particularly dirty, and he wasn't an alcoholic or a druggie. So, I talked to him about this and that.

His name was Morris (or Moses). So, I said to him, "Do you believe in God?" I remember to this day—it was on Columbus Avenue in San Francisco. I looked at him and he had startling blue eyes. He looked at me and said, as though in astonishment, "Why? Who created you?" In that instant, I had a satori, like the Japanese talk about. I understood more completely than I ever had through any preacher or rabbi what it was all about.

Follow it back: "Do you believe in God?" I say to the itinerant man.

He says, stunned, "Why? Who created you?"

I got it in that flash—you know, that flash of understanding; the satori?

Follow it back. So you're an atheist and you say, "Well, how do you know there's a God?" So what is there, nothing? So nothing created you? So you believe in nothing? Therefore, you believe in something—but that's nothing. You believe in nothingness.

I believe in God. That's all. How can you believe in nothingness? How is it possible to believe in nothingness? How can something come from nothing? It's a violation of all the laws of physics! Something cannot come from nothing. It violates physical science, biological science, theological science. It violates all the laws of reason! It violates all the laws of nonreason. So, what I'm getting at is what I learned from that man.

So then I said, "Can I drop you off where you're going?" I drove him to a freeway overpass that no longer exists. The man got out and said good-bye. He disappeared, and I never saw him again. Who was he? A prophet? Was he a reincarnation of a religious figure? I don't know what he was. Maybe he was just a smart guy who was a bum. A lot of bums are smart, and a lot of corporate guys are not that smart. They play people for fools. They think that everybody is a fool because they control the money.

What they don't understand is that there are values beyond money. They've never learned that. Unfortunately, our government is exactly the same. It's MBA all the way, right up into the military hierarchy. They think that an MBA makes them a war hero or a sage, but many would take a pound of flesh or sell their country out for less than thirty pieces of silver. They would teach their children Chinese and move to Shanghai if they had a better offer!

FORTY-FIVE

CONVERSATIONS WITH MY GREAT GRANDFATHER

JUST THE OTHER DAY, I GOT A PICTURE OF A DAGUERREOTYPE of my great grandfather from Russia. It turns out there's a distant relative somewhere in America who's doing the genealogy of the family. I never met my great grandfather. I knew he had to exist. I wouldn't be here without him, God bless him. His name was Laveuc Itzak Vayner, born 1866. In this picture, I see a man in a rabbi's outfit with a suit and tie staring at me. It looks like he has a red beard.

I got the picture of my great grandfather and I started to have conversations with him in my head because there are cultures on earth that believe that their ancestors are with them at all times watching them, watching their every act, and it's what keeps the believers in check. Those of us who carry around our ancestors in our heads are those who keep the human race sane and alive.

As you know, I spent many years collecting medicinal plants on very rare islands of the South Pacific, and I'm talking a long time ago before tourism overtook these areas. And I used to collect primitive art. You can't find primitive art anymore. It's all in museums. And most of these ancestral pieces of art—for example, from New Guinea or New Britain or New Ireland—at that time, contained figures that codified the ancestry of that person. The artist would carve something out of the tree trunk and there would be ancestral faces and bodies in it because they understood quite well that none of us were born unto ourselves. We were all born of a mother who was born of a mother who was born of a mother who was born of a mother who was born of a mother, ad infinitum. So if you forget that chain, that you're part of this human chain of evolution within your own family, what you become is a narcissist without past or future, and, frankly, an empty present.

Something happened in me when I looked at the picture of the great grandfather who I never met. He's staring right at me through this daguerreotype taken around 1860 or 1870. Somewhere in Russia or Poland—somewhere where almost every Jewish person who was left behind was annihilated and killed either by the Nazis or by the Russians.

Since I got this picture, I've been having imaginary conversations with my great grandfather and it has altered my behavior in some ways because I realize I'm not here alone. I didn't come out of the air. I wasn't born through spontaneous combustion. Even as a little boy, I must say, when I was doing naughty stuff, I would apologize to my ancestors. And I would look up and I would think they were there. I would do the naughty stuff anyway because I had no impulse control as a little boy. And I felt they looked away in shame. But more recently, I started to talk to my great grandfather.

So here he is and he looked at me and I looked at him and I imagined the following:

He spoke to me in Hebrew and he said, "Her zuch hein, Michael"—"Listen, Michael." Then he said, "Vus machs du, Michael,"—"What do you do? What are you doing?"

So I said, "I'm a writer and I'm on the radio."

"What's the radio?"

"I talk to a lot of people on the radio."

"What do you say to the people on the radio?"

"I talk about politics and events."

"And what do you say about politics and events?"

"Whatever's going on, I give them my opinion."

"And why is your opinion so important?"

"I don't know. People seem to like the way I think about these things."

"Well, what do you think about these things?"

"Well, Grandfather, it depends upon the situation. For example, if there's a war, maybe I'm against the war."

"And they think what you think is important?"

"Yes."

"Why?"

"Well, they think I have intelligence and I have an education."

"And they don't?" he says.

I say, "No, most people don't have much intelligence, Grandfather, not in the world in which we live. And many people don't have higher educations and they don't know how to think."

"And how do you know how to think?"

"Well, Grandfather, you may not know this but I have a lot of years learning how to think, going all the way back to college. I have many higher degrees where I was taught how to think."

"What do you mean you were taught how to think? You couldn't think when you were a little boy?"

"No, not like I do now. Your grandson, my father, Ben, also taught me how to think."

"And how's that?"

"He taught me how to put two and two together."

"What do you mean two and two together? What's two and two?"

"I learned how to add two and two is four, not six."

"What do you mean, you know how to put things to-gether for people because they can't on their own?"

"Yes."

"So in that sense, you're like a rabbi, like a leader, like a teacher who tries to explain things to people?"

"Uh, I guess so."

So Grandfather said, "Okay, that I can understand. So if you can do that like a rabbi, why aren't you a rabbi?"

"Because I'm not. I don't want to do it through a holy book."

"Why? It worked for me and everyone preceding me for a thousand years or more. Five thousand years we used the holy book. You can't use the holy book? You're too good for it?"

"I don't know, it just seems remote to me, Grandfather. It just seems like these prayers about a being in the sky."

"Why, you don't think He exists? Are you sure of that? Are you sure that your every breath is not because of Him? You're sure that every morsel of bread that you eat every day is not because of Him, every glass of wine that you take is not because of Him?"

I said, "Well, of course I understand the prayer, which is 'God, thank you for giving us the grape and the wine,' and 'thank you for giving me this bread.' I understand all of that, and sometimes I forget it."

"Well, don't forget it," he said to me.

"Why shouldn't I forget it?"

"Because if you forget it, He will forget you. And if He forgets you, you're liable to wind up with nothing."

"You mean, like the Bible says, it will all dry up?"

"It could dry up. Maybe you have everything right now because you do remember Him. Maybe you have everything right now because you still think about him every second."

"Who's Him?"

"Come on. Stop giving me the B.S., Michael. You know what I'm saying. Don't be a wise guy now, you're too old for it," he says to me.

I said, "Okay, so Grandfather, let's go further."

"Further? Where do you want to go?"

"As far as you're going to go."

"You were led back to where you started, which is with God."

"And what should I do now?"

"Do what you're doing. But you're not happy anyway."

"Why?"

"Because you don't talk to God directly. You make believe you do, but you don't. You really want to, but you don't know how to."

"Why don't I know how to?"

"Because you're not leading a clean life."

"Why am I not leading a clean life?"

"Because you're living in a place and a time and a world where there's very little cleanliness. Everything is distorted. Everything is dirty from the point of view of your people. Your people were so pure, your people were so clean that they died for it. Do you know what that means, Michael?"

"I don't want to know."

"Well, no, you shouldn't know. But they died holding the Torah. They'd rather die than not believe in God. And you make believe it's not a big deal. You make believe you could or you could not. When it's convenient for you, you do. You write a book on it because you think you can sell a book?"

"Grandfather, don't be cynical."

"I'm not being cynical. I'm just telling you. Do you really believe what you write or you write it just to make a living?"

"I write it so that people respect me."

"Oh, so you do it for your ego?"

"Well, the Christians say, 'All is vanity.'"

"All right, so the Christians are right. All is vanity. So you're a vain man."

"Yes, I'm a vain man."

"You're only a vain man?"

"I don't know. Let God judge whether I'm only a vain man."

"Are you doing more harm than good or more good than harm?"

"God'll have to judge."

"Oh, the God that you're not sure exists? The God that you mock? The God that you play with?"

"Look, Grandfather, you're putting me in a hard place."

"Yeah, that's where I want you to be. You don't have that much time on earth to play around with these things and these ideas. Either you're all in or don't be in at all. Move to LA, act like one of the other seventy-five-year-old, eighty-year-old schmucks, get yourself a twenty-five-year-old girlfriend and, you know, drive around like you're twenty-five years old. Take Viagra every day and think that you're twenty-five years old, which you're not. Live in that dream world, because that too will come to an end."

"So what do you want me to do, Grandfather?"

"Do what you're doing but do it a little more seriously. Understand that you were put here for a reason and in some regard, you have fulfilled your purpose. In other regards, you're taking it in a little too cavalier a manner. See, I know some words. We knew them in Russian and Hebrew too. We know what cavalier means. You don't really take yourself seriously enough, Michael. I'm trying to tell you that you're way past what even you think you are. You're much more important than you think you are and the reason you don't know who you are is because you don't want to know who you are. And the reason you don't want to know who you are is because you're afraid to know who you are."

"Why am I afraid to know who I am?"

"Why? Because you'll have to change your life and you'll have to do things that you don't want to do."

"Which is what?"

"Lead people for the good of God, for the good of the world."

"I think I have to stop here, Grandfather."

"Why? You're afraid?"

"I'm not afraid. I'm just not sure what you're talking about."

"Well, you want to know what I'm talking about? I'll tell you what I'm talking about. You have to lead people in a more divine manner. You have to lead them in a more holy manner. You have to understand that this is not an accident what you have, having helped elect a president and having conversations with the leader of the most powerful nation on earth. Every word that you say has a power. Each word is an atomic bomb. Do you understand what you release when you talk on the radio or you write a book? Or do you think it's a joke?"

"I think I have to take a break and have a drink now."

"Why? You don't have the strength to go on?"

"I'm not sure if I do. And I don't know if the recording is still recording."

"Oh, that's a good excuse. So why don't you take a break and see if it's still recording because I can keep talking since I'm dead. I'm in the next world. I have nothing to do. See, I'm in eternity. I could talk forever. But you, apparently, you already ran out of steam."

I looked at him and I said, "Okay, Grandfather, what would you have me talk about today to millions of people?"

So far, I haven't received an answer, so I'm going to turn to you with a question. What would my great grandfather want me to talk about today to millions of people? I could tell you that I don't know. What would you have me talk about when you think about all the subjects under the sun? All the subjects under the sun and we're going to talk about four subjects? Mueller and Comey now? Or someone on Fox News?

Do you have conversations with deceased ancestors or would you think you're crazy if you did? Would you call a psychiatrist if you thought you were talking to a deceased ancestor who talked to you with wisdom? Well, you'd probably call a doctor who's a bigger nut than you are to put you on medication and tell you, "Don't even have those conversations because you don't know where it might lead."

I don't care what your race is or your ethnicity or your background, I'm sure there are people who can relate to what I am saying. And if not, well, you're out of luck because this is what I'm going to talk about. I could talk about immigration until I'm blue in the face. You know why? Because I'm an immigrant's son. And in fact, I have the manifest of passengers from the ship that they took coming over to America, landing here in 1920. My grand-mother came with five or six children. Their names are on the List or Manifest of Alien Passengers for the United States. Can you believe this?

You know how powerful this is to be an immigrant's son in a time where immigration is such a hot topic? It gives me a very special view of the subject on both sides of that particular straddle.

And so there are the names. Grandpa came first. He worked for seven years and sent money home to bring over the others; he got them out just before everyone was killed in the village and the country who was not of a certain race or religion. And you think about this, fate and what fate is. They were so poor, as the story came down to me, that they lived in a little village where there was no heat except, of course, from fire. There was a large clay oven in the middle of this room and the older ones would sleep on top of the clay oven to keep from freezing to death. The younger ones would huddle together. And that's why we're strong people. That's why I haven't caved despite the pressure of my life. And every time I start to whine to myself about how tough things are, I remember them.

And by remembering them, I realize how easy I have it and how soft our lives are. And I ask myself and I ask my great grandfather, "Once again I ask you, what would you, Great Grandfather, want for me to talk about today to millions of people? What is worthy of my time on these airways? What would my great grandfather who I never met want for me to talk about to millions of people?"

All through my life, I would do certain things and I would really feel my ancestors looking at me. I would dismiss it thinking, "Ah, they're not real. It doesn't matter what that old person thought." And I would go on and be the ordinary guy that I was. But as I've gotten on in life I've come to realize that maybe it's not so imaginary. After all, they did exist. And maybe we suppress these ideas because we're not living in a world that respects the wisdom of the ages. Instead, we extol the wisdom of idiots in high school, the wisdom of morons who know nothing; they're supposed to lead us now. I just love all the Leftists who say "look at the young people." What the hell do they have to teach us? They learn from the old.

Now, my great grandfather would probably say, "Michael, you can't fight what's going on in the world endlessly. The time clock—listen to the metronome in your head, Michael. Is this how you want to spend the rest of your days, talking about the slime of the earth? Do you want to talk about them for the rest of your life? Is this what you were born for? Is this why God made you a man-child in the promised land? Is this how you're supposed to spend the rest of your days?"

Do you have conversations with yourself? Whether you're a Texan or an Oklahoman on a range, whether you're a guy who herds cattle or drives a tank in battle, do you ever think about these things? Or am I the last person on earth who even thinks about this? But my great grandfather would say, "Michael, that's not what you should be talking about."

So I said, "What should I be talking about, writing about?"

"What do you write about?"

"Well, my last book was God, Faith, and Reason, Grandfather."

He said, "Good. What do you know about God that others don't? You know more about God than the thousand years or five thousand years of people who've studied this subject? You know more than them?" he said to me.

And I said, "No, I don't know more. I only know what I know."

"Well, why would anyone want to know what you know? You're not a scholar of the subject."

"Well, Grandfather, apparently an awful lot of them did because it became a huge bestseller."

"What's a bestseller? We never heard of such a thing in

my world. We didn't buy books because they were bestsell-ers. We didn't read books because they were bestsellers."

"What did you read, Grandfather?"

"We only read one book, the Torah. That's all we read. We read it over and over and over and over again."

I said, "Okay, fine. I'm not knocking it. But we have gone past that book."

"Oh, you have? And what has it led to in the world, that you've gone past it?"

My answer to him was, "What has just reading that one book taken us to in this world when you consider that hundreds of thousands, if not millions, of people have been killed in the name of that one book?"

"I don't like hearing that."

"Well, you don't have to hear it, but it happens to be true. There are people right now killing their own co-religionists in the name of that one book."

"That's not a very good thing, Great Grandson," he said.

My great grandfather looked at me and said, "What is this crazy music you're playing. I never heard anything like this."

"Well, I'm living in America now, the year 2019. We play music like this."

"This is music? You call this music? This is a mishmash of the mind. What music? I never heard anything like this."

"Look, Grandfather, knock it off. Leave me alone, would you, please? An engine on a plane blew last night."

"What's an engine? What's a plane?"

"It's a thing that flies in the sky."

"What, it's a bird? Like a chicken on a Friday night?"

"No, no, no, it flies in the air, carries people."

"Have you gone crazy in the new world? What do you mean that it's something that carries people? I never heard of such a thing in the world I was in."

"Well, Grandfather, I'm trying to tell you something. The engine blew up on this plane and it sucked a woman almost out of the plane and a guy in a cowboy hat pulled her back in."

"Cowboy hat? What's a cowboy hat?"

"And the pilot, they say, has nerves of steel."

"What's a nerve of steel?"

"She's a Navy pilot."

"What's a Navy pilot?"

Anyway, the fact is, if you play with this game for a while, it becomes fun to do it in several dimensions at once because it keeps you from going insane, talking about the news.

FORTY-SIX

THE KNOCKOUT

HE WAS FLATTENED BEFORE HE WAS BORN. HE DIDN'T HAVE a chance. His cowardly, small father used to tell him a story when he was a little boy about a farmer who lifted up a calf, from the time it was born, over his head. He would look at his son as they walked in the ghetto and tell him about the farmer who lifted up the calf over his head. And as the calf grew, he was able to lift it up when it was a full-grown bull. The little boy didn't know what the small father was telling him. He thought it was just a story about a farmer. Little did he know that his sadistic father was telling him that the boy was the young calf who he would lift over his head so when the boy became a bull, he would still be a malleable calf.

As years went on, the father continued to pick on him, ridicule him, bully him, everything he could do to make him small, to keep him under control. As the boy became a teenager, he found out he liked music and he picked up a flute that he would secretly practice in the basement of their little house. He grew his hair long. He wore black clothing. He would fly away on the flute's notes. Then, one day, the father came down in the basement and saw his son doing the unimaginable: playing the flute. Well, he went crazy, screaming at him, calling him every name under the sun. The boy never picked up the flute again.

As boys will, he wanted to please his father. He knew his father was a boxing fan because every Friday night, they'd watch the Friday night fights on TV. So the boy, who was small of frame but strong of spirit, decided he would learn how to box. He secretly got a book on boxing and, for over a year, he would practice boxing moves in his tiny bedroom. It was an interesting art to him, all the different angles of the punches. And he practiced and practiced and practiced, shadowboxing in his little room.

Eventually, his uncle came into his life and was going to help him actually learn how to box. His father's brother had a black friend who was a light-heavyweight contender training for a big fight at Yankee Stadium. The fighter's name was Archie. One day, the boy's uncle arranged for the thin, small kid to meet Archie in his father's store.

The boy was awed by him. He was tall and strong, but he was kind and gentle. He was friendly, not condescending. He said to the skinny boy, "Okay, you can come up to my gym in Harlem," which was the most famous black boxing gym in his time, and still is—the Salem Crescent Athletic Club (SCAC). Archie wore a jacket that said SCAC. And the kid knew that one day he'd wear that jacket—at least, he thought so. So the big black man said to the small white boy, "You'll come up by train. It will be a long train ride, but I'll teach you how to fight. You'll need to get some gym clothes. You'll need to get a cup." The boy turned red with embarrassment. Just the word "cup" embarrassed him, and the thought of him mentioning a jockstrap— that's the kind of shyness the boy had at the time. And so the boy and his uncle made preparations for him to take his first boxing lesson up in Harlem. Well, when the mean father heard about it, he screamed at him in a tirade. "Are you crazy? You're gonna get your head busted open." That was the end of his boxing career.

So he couldn't play the flute and he couldn't box. What was left for him to do?

FORTY-SEVEN

God's Warriors

PRESENTED DECEMBER 1, 2018, AT THE SPECIAL
FORCES CHRISTMAS PARTY, BENICIA YACHT CLUB

NOT WEARING THE RED BADGE OF COURAGE, I'M HUMBLED
speaking tonight before you, who are God's warriors.
How can I, a man who's never felt the blade or the bullet
begin to understand the world of those like you who have?

What I do understand and think I might share with
you is my love for America. As an immigrant's son, the
grandson of Sam who fled the Reds of Russia, I am truly a
man-child in the promised land, but we are all now facing
a new wave of committed Marxist revolutionaries who

detest the American way and vow to tear down all that is good and fair and replace it with evil and unfairness.

Pardon me for being a little political tonight, but I have no way around it. It's all I can do. It's all I can think about. Taking from those who created and built up to redistribute to those who gave nothing but hatred and destruction, and behind these hardened, aging, communist revolutionaries is a new generation. A new generation of ignorance and platitudes. Nice children walking into a den of hyenas.

How do we go forward when our warnings have been made to sound quaint and even antique? Our words and wisdom mocked, ridiculed, and crucified daily by the legions of the deceit peddlers where fake news and fake history is sold by fake heroes leading us to becoming a fake nation. The long history of western civilization, tied as it is to Christianity, has now been assaulted so that all of its greatness is now tainted with doubt and second-guessing. Where even great religions' art, envision the Sistine Chapel ceiling by Michelangelo, is mocked by those who could not hold a palette to even a journeyman painter at that time.

Where those who write with a vocabulary of 50,000 words of English are ridiculed. Where those who do higher mathematics are insulted in our schools by those who cannot add two columns of three figures. How do good warriors stand and take this abuse? I'll quote from Rudyard Kipling's, "If." "If you can keep your head when all about you / Are losing theirs and blaming it on you, / If you can trust yourself when all men doubt you, / But make allowance for their doubting too; . . . /Or being hated, don't give way to hating, / And yet don't look too good, nor talk too wise. . . . / If you can talk with crowds and keep your virtue, / Or walk with Kings—nor lose the common touch," that's how you do it.

I came here tonight to tell you that you are not alone. You are supported by most Americans. Although the fake radical news and the biased social media may not support you, I will tell you the silent majority does and there are more of us than there are of them. If it was not for you heroes and your fallen brothers, we would not be here today. The spiteful communist radicals who put us all down would not have the platform they stand on to spew their hatred. They would be living in the nightmares that they promote, never knowing how great their lives are in the now and how great this country is because of you.

Keep this message alive. Share it with all the soldiers that you know who may not have heard in a long time how thankful America is for the sacrifices they have made. I thank you, the Savage Nation thanks you, America thanks you. God bless America, borders, language, culture.

ACKNOWLEDGMENTS

For various family photographs, I would like to thank Sheila Weiner and Sam Furgang.

CREDITS AND NOTES

Chapters 18–45 previously appeared in the self-published volume *Psychological Nudity* (2008).

Chapters 45–47 © 2019 by Michael Savage.

Thanks to Thomas Nelson Publishers for permission to reprint the following stories:

From *The Enemy Within* by Michael Savage (Nelson Current, 2003): "Dead Man's Pants," pp. 7–8 and "Fat Pat & Tippy the Dog."

From *Liberalism Is a Mental Disorder* by Michael Savage (Nelson Current, 2005): "Sam the Butcher."

Disclaimer: All articles retain the original copyrights of their original owners.

Notes

p. 191 "Monkeys Rampage in Indian Capital," *AFP*, November 12, 2007.

p. 229 "U.S. Couples Seek Separate Bedrooms," *BBC News*, March 12, 2007. http://news.bbc.co.uk/2/hi/americas/6441131.stm.

p. 232 Martinfield, Sean. "Nan Kempner—American Chic." *The San Francisco Sentinel*, June 28, 2007.

p. 242 Buddha. *Teaching of Buddha*. Bukkyo Dendo Kyokai (BDK).

BOOKS BY MICHAEL SAVAGE

TRICKLE DOWN TYRANNY
CRUSHING OBAMA'S DREAM OF THE SOCIALIST STATES OF AMERICA

"A how-to guide on fixing our national crisis. . . . A damning critique not only of the Obama administration but also the half of the population that put him in office and still supports his devastating policies."

—*Washington Times*

TRICKLE UP POVERTY
STOPPING OBAMA'S ATTACK ON OUR BORDERS, ECONOMY, AND SECURITY

"A blazing flamethrower of truth, Michael Savage pulls no punches and goes right for the jugular with facts, not vacuous hyperbole."

—Ted Nugent, *Washington Times*

A SAVAGE LIFE

"Savage recalls his childhood growing up in the Bronx. . . . He's got the knack for evocative detail, and this series of short vignettes features some indelible images, such as the immigrant father who, insisting that nothing be wasted, forced his son to wear dead men's trousers."

—*Washington Post*

HarperCollins*Publishers*

DISCOVER GREAT AUTHORS, EXCLUSIVE OFFERS, AND MORE AT HC.COM.